The Fundamentals of Job Coaching

Strategies, tools and resources for Job Coaches

First published in the United States in 2025.

Author: Rosie Lovato

ISBN: 9781736438534

Discounts on bulk quantities are available to qualified organizations. For details and specific discount information, contact information available on www.rivergardensec.com

---

DEDICATION

To my children, who have been my motivation to continue learning and aspire for more. To my dear friends who have supported me from the beginning. And to those who have answered the call to serve the most vulnerable.

Introduction

The Fundamentals of Job Coaching is designed for current and aspiring job coaches dedicated to empowering others on their journeys toward meaningful employment. Job coaching goes beyond merely helping someone find a job; it involves guiding individuals toward confidence, independence, and personal growth. Whether your clients come from the general public or belong to specific groups—such as youth, individuals with disabilities, justice-involved individuals, veterans, or those in recovery—this book equips you with the knowledge, tools, and insights needed to make a lasting impact.

This comprehensive guide explores what it takes to become a successful job coach. We delve into common employment barriers clients may face and provide effective strategies to help them overcome these challenges. Each chapter offers valuable resources, best practices, and real-world strategies tailored to the evolving needs of today's job market.

Throughout this book, you'll gain a deeper understanding of the job coach's role, discover practical methods for assessing and enhancing clients' skills, and learn techniques for building rapport and fostering resilience. As you embark on this journey, you'll find that job coaching is a dynamic and rewarding field where compassion meets strategy, and every interaction holds the potential to create meaningful change.

Let this book serve as your guide, supporting you as you empower others and helping you become an impactful mentor in your clients' pursuit of opportunity and self-sufficiency.

CONTENTS

1

Job Coaching

- The Job Coach
- Training and Qualifications
- Roles and Responsibilities
- Job Settings
- Ethical Considerations
- Professional Standards
- Establishing Rapport and Trust
- The Coach-Client Agreement
- Preventing Burnout
- Resources for Job Coaches

There are various types of coaches, but the core purpose of any coach is to provide individuals with guidance, support, and strategies to achieve their personal or professional goals. Coaches help clients identify their strengths, overcome obstacles, and develop actionable plans to reach their desired outcomes. By offering a non-judgmental and motivating environment, coaches empower clients to gain clarity on their goals, build confidence, and maintain accountability. This support is essential for helping clients navigate challenges and break negative patterns.

THE JOB COACH

The role of a job coach is multifaceted, intersecting with both human services and social services. It involves providing comprehensive support to individuals seeking employment. Job coaches play a crucial role in their clients' success in the job market, helping them achieve career goals and maintain sustainable employment.

Job coaches empower individuals to take control of their career paths and achieve self-sufficiency. They promote inclusivity by assisting marginalized populations—such as people with disabilities or those with a history of substance use—in gaining meaningful employment. By helping individuals secure jobs, job coaches contribute to reducing unemployment rates and enhancing the economic well-being of communities.

A job coach working with individuals who belong to multiple intersecting marginalized groups—such as veterans with disabilities who are also justice-impacted—must adopt a holistic and individualized approach. This involves conducting a comprehensive assessment to understand each client's unique challenges and strengths, addressing multiple barriers simultaneously.

In these situations, job coaches should leverage specialized resources and support systems tailored to each aspect of the client's background, including disability accommodations, veteran services, and re-entry programs. Effective coordination with various agencies and community organizations is crucial for providing integrated support.

Additionally, the job coach should foster an inclusive, empathetic environment, advocating for clients' needs and promoting resilience and self-efficacy. By understanding and addressing the complex interplay of factors affecting each client, the job coach can create a personalized plan that enhances employment prospects and supports overall well-being.

Being a job coach is both challenging and rewarding. Challenges can arise when working with clients who face significant barriers to employment, such as lack of experience, disabilities, or past incarceration. These situations require a deep understanding of each client's unique needs and the development of tailored strategies to support them. Navigating these complexities, advocating for necessary accommodations, and maintaining patience and persistence can be demanding.

However, the rewards are substantial. Job coaches witness their clients' personal and professional growth, help them secure meaningful employment, and contribute to their increased self-confidence and independence. The satisfaction of making a tangible difference in someone's life and the joy of seeing clients succeed and thrive in their careers make this role immensely fulfilling.

TRAINING AND QUALIFICATIONS

The path to becoming a job coach is diverse, encompassing formal education, hands-on experience, and professional development opportunities. Some employers hire individuals with skills well suited to coaching, while others prefer candidates with prior experience in fields such as human services, social work, education, or vocational rehabilitation.

Online Courses

Online platforms such as Coursera, Udemy, and LinkedIn Learning may offer courses in career coaching, job development, and related fields.

These courses provide a flexible option for individuals looking to gain foundational knowledge or specialize in specific areas.

Workshops and Seminars

Various organizations—such as workforce development agencies, nonprofits, and professional coaching associations—offer short-term workshops and seminars that focus on specific aspects of job coaching, including working with special populations or understanding labor market trends.

Professional Organizations

Organizations like the National Career Development Association (NCDA) and the International Coach Federation (ICF) offer specialized training and certification programs for career and job coaches. These programs typically combine coursework, mentoring, and supervised practice.

Workforce Development Programs

Some government-sponsored workforce development programs provide training for job coaches as part of their employment services. These programs often focus on assisting specific populations, such as veterans, individuals with disabilities, or those transitioning from incarceration.

On-the-Job Training

Many job coaches gain training through on-the-job experience, often starting in roles related to human services, social work, or career counseling. Employers may offer in-house training or mentoring to help new job coaches develop the skills necessary for success in their roles.

Mentorship and Peer Learning

Aspiring job coaches can also learn through mentorship and peer learning, collaborating with experienced coaches who offer guidance, feedback, and practical insights into the coaching process.

Formal Training for Job Coaches

Various educational institutions offer certificate programs in job coaching, career development, or vocational counseling. These programs typically cover key topics such as career assessment, job search strategies, resume writing, and interview preparation.

George Washington University, Graduate Certificate in the Foundations of Rehabilitation Counseling

https://gsehd.gwu.edu

National Career Development Association (NCDA), Facilitating Career Development (FCD) Training

https://ncda.org

The International Association of Career Coaches, Career Coach Certifications

https://www.iacareercoaches.org

The Center for Credentialing & Education, Inc., Global Career Development Facilitator (GCDF)
https://www.cce-global.org

University of California, San Diego Extension (UCSD), Career Advising Program

https://extendedstudies.ucsd.edu/courses-and-programs/career-advising

New York University (NYU) School of Professional Studies, Career and Life Planning courses

https://bulletins.nyu.edu/courses/

National Employment Counseling Association (NECA), Global Career Development Facilitator

https://www.employmentcounseling.org/global-career-development-facilitator-gcdf-us-cce-approved-provider.html

Occupational Profiles

School and Career Counselors and Advisors
https://www.bls.gov/ooh/community-and-social-service/school-and-career-counselors.htm

Educational, Guidance, and Career Counselors and Advisors
https://www.onetonline.org

ROLES AND RESPONSIBILITIES

Roles

Facilitator: Mediating between the client and potential employers, ensuring effective communication and understanding.

Advisor: Offering expert guidance on job search strategies, career planning, and professional development.

Mentor: Providing mentorship to help clients develop skills, set goals, and navigate the job market.

Supporter: Offering emotional and motivational support, helping clients build confidence and resilience.

Advocate: Championing clients' needs and accommodations in the workplace, ensuring fair treatment and equal opportunities.

Trainer: Leading training sessions on essential job-related skills, including resume writing, interview techniques, and workplace etiquette.

Responsibilities

- Client Assessment and Goal Setting
- Developing Individualized Plans
- Resume and Cover Letter Assistance
- Job Search Support
- Assistance with Interview Preparation
- Workplace Integration and Support
- Skill Development
- Assistance with overcoming Barriers

- Networking and Relationship Building
- Ongoing Monitoring and Support
- Employer Engagement
- Documentation and Reporting
- Compliance and Confidentiality
- Professional Development

Skills

General skills job coaches should possess:

Soft Skills

- Active listening
- Empathy
- Communication
- Goal-setting
- Problem-solving
- Patience
- Adaptability
- Cultural competence
- Time management
- Collaboration
- Coaching and mentoring
- Critical thinking
- Resourcefulness
- Organization
- Motivational interviewing
- Conflict resolution
- Networking

Hard Skills

- Computer skills and digital literacy
- Knowledge of labor market trends
- Documentation and record-keeping
- Career assessment tools
- Resume and document formatting
- Research skills

At a minimum, job coaches should have a general understanding of current labor market trends, job outlooks, educational requirements, and local resources. This includes knowledge of nearby schools (e.g., colleges, vocational programs), community resources, and local employers, as well as the ability to assist with job-ready tasks such as applications and resumes.

"In my experience as a Career Coach, I think the greatest skills to have are: case management skills, resourcefulness, problem-solving, good communication, time management, and the ability to stay organized." - Rosie Lovato

Techniques

Coaches may need to utilize various techniques, such as motivational interviewing, cognitive-behavioral strategies, and accountability measures, to help clients make sustainable changes. This approach, structured yet adaptable, ensures clients stay focused, motivated, and on track to achieve their desired outcomes.

JOB SETTINGS

Job coaches can work in various settings and may hold titles such as Job Coach, Career Coach, Career Counselor, Case Manager, or similar roles. Regardless of the title, their focus remains on supporting individuals in career development and achieving employment goals.

- Community Job / Career Centers
- Educational Institutions / Schools
- Community Centers
- Nonprofit Organizations

- Employment Agencies
- Healthcare and Rehabilitation Facilities
- Social Services Organizations
- Correctional Facilities
- Vocational Rehabilitation Centers
- Government Agencies
- Private Companies
- Freelance / Private Practice

If you work at a community job center, you may assist a diverse range of clients, offering guidance and support to individuals from various backgrounds with different needs. Alternatively, some job coaches specialize in specific populations, such as individuals with disabilities, veterans, recent graduates, or those re-entering the workforce after a long absence. These specialized coaches tailor their services to address the unique challenges and opportunities faced by their target groups. The advantage of working with specific populations is that job coaches can gain a deeper understanding of the common needs and barriers their clients face, enabling them to offer more effective and targeted assistance.

ETHICAL CONSIDERATIONS

Job coaches must adhere to ethical considerations and professional standards to provide effective, respectful, and responsible services. By upholding these standards, they foster trust and promote positive outcomes in clients' career development.

Confidentiality: Always maintain client confidentiality. Do not disclose personal information without the client's explicit consent, except when required by law. Securely store all client records and data to prevent unauthorized access.

Informed Consent: Ensure clients understand the nature, scope, and potential outcomes of the coaching relationship. Obtain informed consent before starting sessions and keep clients informed of any changes in the coaching process.

Professional Boundaries: Maintain clear professional boundaries to avoid conflicts of interest or dual relationships. Avoid personal relationships with clients that could impair professional judgment or risk exploitation.

Competence: Provide services within the boundaries of your expertise, based on your education, training, and experience. Seek supervision, additional training, or refer clients to other professionals when issues fall outside your scope of competence.

Respect and Non-Discrimination: Treat all clients with respect, dignity, and fairness, regardless of background, beliefs, or personal characteristics. Avoid discrimination or bias in service delivery.

Transparency: Be transparent about your qualifications, fees, and services. Provide clear and accurate information about what clients can expect from the coaching process.

Integrity: Act with honesty and integrity in all professional interactions. Avoid deceptive practices or misrepresentation of qualifications or services.

Client Autonomy: Respect clients' autonomy and their right to make their own decisions. Support them in setting their own goals and taking responsibility for their career development. Be mindful of the potential impact of your advice and actions on their lives.

PROFESSIONAL STANDARDS

To provide effective job coaching, it is essential to adhere to professional practices and ethical standards.

Ongoing Professional Development: Stay up to date with the latest trends, techniques, and best practices in job coaching by participating in relevant training, workshops, and professional associations.

Client-Centered Approach: Focus on the individual needs, strengths, and aspirations of each client. Encourage client participation and feedback to ensure a collaborative and empowering coaching process.

Supervision and Peer Feedback: Seek guidance and feedback from supervisors and peers, especially when dealing with challenging cases.

Ethical Decision-Making: Utilize an ethical decision-making framework when faced with dilemmas or challenging situations.

Accurate Record-Keeping: Maintain detailed and accurate records of all coaching sessions, including goals, progress, and significant issues discussed. Ensure documentation is factual, respectful, and up to date.

Collaboration: Work with other professionals to provide comprehensive support for clients.

Clear Communication: Communicate clearly and respectfully with clients, colleagues, and other stakeholders.

Professional Conduct: Maintain professionalism in all interactions, including punctuality, preparedness, and adherence to an appropriate dress code.

Legislative Awareness: Stay informed about changes in legislation that may impact your practice or clients.

Compliance and Accountability: Comply with all relevant laws, regulations, and organizational policies related to job coaching and employment services.

ESTABLISHING RAPPORT AND TRUST

Building rapport and trust with clients is crucial for job coaches to establish supportive and effective coaching relationships. By implementing the following strategies, job coaches can create a solid foundation for successful and collaborative coaching experiences.

Active Listening: Focus entirely on the client, avoiding distractions to demonstrate full engagement in the conversation. Reflect on the client's statements and paraphrase to show understanding and validate their feelings and thoughts.

Empathy and Understanding: Show genuine care and understanding of the client's situation and goals. Validate their experiences and challenges without judgment.

Consistency and Reliability: Maintain reliability by keeping appointments, following through on commitments, and being punctual. Provide consistent guidance and support throughout the coaching process.

Open and Honest Communication: Clearly explain your role, the coaching process, and what clients can expect. Foster an environment where clients feel safe to express their thoughts and concerns.

Respect and Non-Judgment: Treat clients with dignity and respect, regardless of their background or circumstances. Approach each client with an open mind, avoiding assumptions or judgments.

Personalized Attention: Tailor your coaching methods to meet the unique needs, goals, and preferences of each client. Acknowledge and appreciate each client's individuality.

Confidentiality: Ensure clients that their personal information and discussions will remain confidential, creating a safe space for open communication.

Positive Reinforcement: Celebrate clients' achievements, no matter how small. Provide positive feedback and encouragement to keep clients motivated.

Building Competence: Help clients recognize their strengths and build confidence. Provide tools, resources, and strategies to help them achieve their goals.

Being Present: Show genuine interest in the client's journey and well-being. Be fully present during coaching sessions, demonstrating that you value their time and effort.

Setting Boundaries: Clearly define and communicate the boundaries of the coaching relationship. Respect the client's boundaries and personal space.

Feedback and Adjustment: Invite clients to provide feedback on the coaching process and make adjustments as needed. Remain flexible and adapt your approach based on client feedback and progress.

Professionalism: Maintain professionalism while balancing approachability. Display your expertise and knowledge in the field to instill confidence in your ability to support clients.

THE COACH-CLIENT AGREEMENT

All coaches should establish a coach-client agreement at the start of services. This formal agreement sets clear expectations, defines roles and responsibilities, and outlines the structure of the coaching relationship. A well-crafted agreement helps prevent misunderstandings and ensures that both the coach and client are aligned in their goals and commitments.

A key component of any coaching agreement is emphasizing the importance of the client's initiative and follow-through. While the coach provides guidance, support, and accountability, the client is ultimately responsible for their progress. Success relies on the client's active engagement in the process, including setting goals, taking steps toward achieving them, and honoring commitments made during sessions.

This initiative is crucial for unlocking the full potential of the coaching relationship, as personal effort and action drive meaningful change and growth. By clearly defining the client's role in the agreement, both parties understand that success depends on the client's dedication to applying what they've learned and consistently working toward their objectives.

Agreement Template

The Coach-Client Agreement

This agreement outlines the expectations, responsibilities, and commitments of both the coach and the client in the coaching relationship. It is intended to foster a successful and productive partnership.

Purpose of Coaching
The purpose of job coaching is to support the client in their job search and career development, helping them identify goals, build skills, and navigate the job market.

Roles and Responsibilities

Coach's' Role:

- Provide personalized coaching, guidance, feedback, resources and support tailored to the client's needs.
- Assist in setting realistic and actionable goals.
- Offer tools, resources, and strategies to enhance the client's job search and career development.
- Maintain confidentiality and create a safe, non-judgmental environment for the client.

Clients' Role:

- Take initiative by actively engaging in the coaching process.
- Set personal goals and work toward achieving them.
- Follow through on agreed-upon actions and commitments between coaching sessions.
- Communicate openly with the coach about progress, challenges, and any changes in priorities.
- Be accountable for their own decisions and actions.

Structure of Coaching Sessions

- Sessions will take place (weekly/bi-weekly/monthly) at a mutually agreed-upon time and will last approximately (duration).
- The format of the sessions will be (in-person/virtual/phone).
- The client will be expected to come prepared for each session, having completed any assignments or action steps agreed upon in the previous session.

Confidentiality
All information shared during the coaching sessions will remain confidential unless the client provides explicit permission to share information, or if required by law (e.g., in cases of potential harm to self or others).

Duration of the Agreement
This agreement will remain in effect for a period of (duration) starting from the date signed below. Either party may terminate the agreement with (notice period) written notice.

Payment and Cancellation Policy

- The cost of each session is (amount), payable (before/after) each session or as agreed upon.
- Cancellations must be made at least (hours/days) in advance, or the client may be charged for the missed session, except in cases of emergency.

Agreement to Terms
By signing this agreement, both the coach and the client agree to uphold the commitments outlined above. This agreement is a shared commitment to creating a productive and meaningful coaching relationship.

PREVENTING BURNOUT

Job coaches, like other frontline workers who engage with the public or special populations, can be susceptible to burnout due to the emotional and logistical demands of their work. Preventing burnout is essential to ensure that both the coach and their clients can achieve their goals in a sustainable and healthy manner.

Here are some best practices for preventing burnout and maintaining energy, enthusiasm, and effectiveness as a job coach.

Set Realistic Expectations

Set achievable and realistic goals for yourself and your clients. Recognize that success varies for each individual, and progress may come in small steps. Working with individuals facing complex barriers to employment can be challenging, especially when progress is slow, or setbacks occur. To maintain motivation and prevent burnout, celebrate incremental victories—for both your clients and you.

Maintain Professional Boundaries

Job coaches who work closely with clients may become emotionally invested, which can lead to compassion fatigue. To prevent this, establish and maintain clear boundaries. While it's essential to show empathy, it's equally important to separate professional and personal involvement. Practice compassionate detachment to avoid absorbing the emotional burdens of your clients' challenges.

Practice Self-Care

Without regular self-care, burnout can quickly set in, especially in emotionally demanding occupations. Engage in activities that replenish your energy and support your physical, emotional, and mental well-being. Regular exercise, mindfulness practices (such as meditation or yoga), hobbies, and social activities outside of work can help rejuvenate your spirit. Additionally, prioritize sleep, healthy eating, and stress-relief techniques to maintain balance and resilience.

Engage in Regular Supervision and Peer Support

Sharing the challenges and successes of your work with peers or a supervisor provides emotional support and practical guidance. Participate in regular supervision sessions or peer support groups to debrief difficult situations, seek advice, and gain new perspectives. Connecting with others who understand your work can help reduce feelings of isolation and frustration.

Take Time Off When Needed

Continuous exposure to the stresses of job coaching, especially when working with vulnerable populations, can lead to emotional exhaustion. Use your vacation and personal days when necessary. Even short breaks or time off can help recharge your energy and improve focus upon your return. Avoid overworking or frequently staying late, as it can contribute to burnout over time.

Develop Strong Time Management Skills

Juggling multiple clients and responsibilities can feel overwhelming if time is not managed effectively. Prioritize tasks, set a schedule, and create clear daily or weekly goals. Use time-blocking techniques or to-do lists to stay organized. This approach helps reduce chaos and allows for more focused attention on each client without feeling rushed or overburdened.

Celebrate Successes and Reflect on Impact

Job coaching can be emotionally taxing, and it's easy to lose sight of the positive impact you're making. Regularly reflect on the positive outcomes of your work. Celebrate successes with your clients and acknowledge progress, no matter how small. Keep a journal or log of client milestones to remind yourself of the meaningful impact you're having.

Seek Continuing Education and Professional Development

Job coaching can be emotionally taxing, and it's easy to lose sight of the positive impact you're making. Regularly reflect on the positive outcomes of your work. Celebrate successes with your clients and acknowledge progress, no matter how small. Keep a journal or log of client milestones to remind yourself of the meaningful impact you're having.

Know When to Refer Clients to Other Services

Job coaches may encounter situations beyond their expertise or capacity, such as serious mental health issues or complex social challenges. Recognize when it's necessary to refer clients to other professionals, such as Academic Advisors, Community Health Workers, Housing Navigators, or legal aid advisors. Acknowledging that you can't solve all problems alone helps prevent overextension and burnout.

Foster a Positive Work Environment

A supportive and positive workplace can significantly reduce stress and the risk of burnout. Foster collaboration and positivity with your colleagues by promoting a culture of mutual support where challenges and achievements are openly shared. Encourage management to provide adequate resources, staffing, and opportunities for professional growth.

RESOURCES FOR JOB COACHES

- Motivational Interviewing https://motivationalinterviewing.org/
- WorkforceGPS https://www.workforcegps.org/

Occupational Information and Data

- Bureau of Labor Statistics www.bls.gov
- ONET Online www.onetonline.org

Associations

- The National Career Development Association (NCDA) https://www.ncda.org/aws/NCDA/pt/sp/home_page
- National Employment Counseling Association (NECA) https://www.employmentcounseling.org/
- International Coaching Federation https://coachingfederation.org/
- National Association of Workforce Development Professionals https://www.nawdp.org/

Online Learning

- Coursera www.cousera.org
- Udemy www.udemy.com
- LinkedIn Learning www.learning.linkedin.com

2

Assessments and Goal Setting

- The Initial Meeting and Assessments
- Setting Goals
- Developing an Action Plan
- Factors that Determine Success
- Resources for Job Coaches

If you've experienced the job search process yourself, you know that finding employment requires effort and strategy. There are job search techniques that can significantly increase a job seeker's chances of gaining employment. However, many clients may not have a solid plan for seeking employment, making the support of a job coach a valuable advantage.

By following a structured approach, coaches help clients navigate their journey from their current state to their desired outcomes, ensuring they remain focused, motivated, and prepared to handle challenges along the way.

The job coaching process typically involves the following steps:

1. Conducting an assessment(s)
2. Developing and setting goals
3. Developing an action plan
4. Provide ongoing support

THE INITIAL MEETING AND ASSESSMENTS

The Initial Meeting

1. Explain Job Readiness:

   During your initial meeting or at the start of job coaching services, explain to your client what it means to be "job-ready."

   This includes being prepared to seek and secure employment, as well as maintaining a job once hired. It also involves the ability to create a resume, complete job applications, write letters to employers, and effectively prepare for interviews. The process requires time, effort, determination, and strategy. To be successful in gaining employment, being resourceful, organized, and persistent is key.

2. Provide a Job Readiness Checklist:

   Provide your clients with a checklist of the basic yet essential items required for job readiness. This allows them to identify what they have and what they need. From there, you can help your client create a tailored plan for gaining employment.

   - ☐ Documents – ID, Social Security Card
   - ☐ Professional Email
   - ☐ Appropriate Social Media
   - ☐ Master Resume
   - ☐ Resume(s)
   - ☐ Master Application
   - ☐ Letters (cover letter, thank you letters, letters of recommendation)
   - ☐ List of References
   - ☐ Interview Skills (how to answer questions)

- ☐ Calendar
- ☐ People/Network Help
- ☐ Application Log
- ☐ Password Log
- ☐ Access to the Internet
- ☐ Work Experience
- ☐ Volunteer Experience
- ☐ Interview Outfit

3. Organize and Retain Essential Materials:

The items you help your client obtain will be valuable not only for their current job search but also as they advance in their career journey. Encourage them to keep everything organized in one place for easy access when needed. Consider providing a folder for storing job leads, resources, templates, and other important documents. This approach fosters better organization and preparedness throughout their employment journey.

... Encourage your client to keep a binder with all the information related to job or career development.

Key Considerations

1. What type of jobs do they want to apply for?

2. Identifying interests, strengths, skills, and areas for improvement.

3. What jobs are they qualified for? (What experience and skills do they have?)

4. Does the client have basic computer skills and a computer? Can the client conduct online job searches, send emails, type letters, submit applications online, etc.?

5. When does the client have time to do their job search?

Knowing these things will let you and your client know where to start looking for job vacancies.

Conducting Client Assessments

A coach cannot effectively assist a client without first assessing their current situation, strengths, weaknesses, and aspirations. This typically involves discussions and self-assessment tools to gain a clear understanding of the client's needs and goals.

Job coaches may use various types of assessments, including needs assessments, career aptitude tests, personality tests, and evaluations for assistive technology. These tools help clients identify their strengths, preferences, and potential career paths that align with their skills and interests. As a job coach, you may facilitate these assessments directly or refer clients to other agencies for additional support.

Some clients may have a clear idea of the type of job they want or their long-term career goals, while others may have limited work experience and be unsure about what they want to do or what jobs they qualify for.

Start by asking your client, "What do you think you want to do?" or "What do you think you'd enjoy doing?" Then, have them take relevant assessments to see if the results align with their initial thoughts. Comparing their interests with the outcomes of personality tests can provide valuable confirmation and help guide the client toward suitable career paths.

Suggest Skill Enhancement

As a coach, you may identify areas where your client could benefit from acquiring specific skills. There are many training options available to help enhance skills and qualifications. Clients can take online courses, attend workshops, or enroll in short-term programs to gain new skills or certifications relevant to their target industry.

Additionally, volunteering or internships can provide valuable hands-on experience and help clients build their resumes. These opportunities not only develop practical skills but also expand professional networks, increasing their chances of securing employment.

Entrepreneurs

If your client is considering starting a business, it's a good idea to refer them to a local Small Business Development Center, Women's Business Center, or Veteran Business Outreach Center.

SETTING GOALS

SMART Goals

Based on the assessment results, the coach can help the client set specific, measurable, attainable, relevant, and time-bound (SMART) goals that align with their vision for the future. SMART Goals is a widely used framework for goal setting, which stands for:

Specific: Goals should be clear and detailed, answering the questions of who, what, where, when, and why.

Measurable: Goals should include a criterion to measure progress and success, helping you track your advancements and stay motivated.

Achievable: Goals should be realistic and attainable, considering available resources and limitations.

Relevant: Goals should align with broader objectives and contribute to your overall plans and purpose.

Time-bound: Goals should have a clear timeline with defined start and end dates, creating a sense of urgency and focus.

Example: *For the next two months, every Wednesday and Thursday afternoon, I will apply for at least one job per day or follow up on applications I've recently submitted. (I will block-out time on my calendar.)*

The GROW Model

Another effective framework for setting goals is the GROW model. Commonly used in coaching and mentoring, this model helps individuals clarify their goals and create actionable plans to achieve them. By following the GROW model, individuals can systematically work through their goals—understanding their current reality, exploring options, and creating a clear path forward to achieve their desired outcomes.

Goal: Define what you want to achieve. The goal should be clear, specific, and aligned with your broader objectives.

What do you want to achieve?
What is the specific outcome you are aiming for?
How will you know when you have achieved it?

Reality: Assess your current situation and understand the context. This involves evaluating where you are now and identifying any obstacles or challenges.

Where do you stand in relation to your goal?
What challenges or obstacles are you facing?
What resources do you have at your disposal?

Options: Explore various strategies and options for achieving the goal. This step involves brainstorming potential solutions and evaluating their feasibility.

What are the possible ways to achieve your goal?
What are the pros and cons of each option?
What resources or support do you need?

Way Forward: Develop a concrete action plan and commit to the steps necessary to achieve the goal. This includes setting timelines and identifying support mechanisms.

What specific actions will you take to move forward?
What is your timeline for each action?
Who can support you, and how will you seek their help?

DEVELOPING ACTION PLANS

Action Plan Development

Once goals are established, the job coach works closely with the client to develop a detailed action plan. This plan outlines the steps necessary to achieve the goals, including both short-term and long-term actions. The job coach helps break down larger objectives into manageable tasks, sets deadlines, and identifies potential obstacles.

Individualized Action Plans should include:

- Current Employment Status
- Desired Career
- Initial Assessment Summary (strengths, areas for development, barriers)
- Short-Term and Long-Term Goals
- Description of Current Situation
- Challenges
- Options for gaining experience and skill development
- Action Plan for 1-3 months, 4-6 months, 7-12 months
- Ongoing Tasks
- List of Support and Resources
- Job Coaching Meeting Schedule
- Progress tracked and recorded

Template for an Individual Coaching/Action Plan

Job Coaching Action Plan
Client Information **Name:** **Age:** **Current Employment Status:** **Desired Career:** **Initial Assessment Summary** **Strengths:** **Areas for Development:** **Barriers:**
Goals **Short-Term Goals** 1. 2. 3.

Reasons for Goals/Motivating Factors:

Long-Term Goals

1.
2.
3.

Reasons for Goals/Motivating Factors:

Reality

Current Situation

Challenges

Options

Skill Development

Practical Experience

Networking and Mentorship

Moving Forward / Action Plan

Month 1-3

Month 4-6

Month 7-12

Ongoing Tasks

Support and Resources

Mentor:

Online Courses:

Networking:

Job Coach:

Plan for Monitoring and Evaluation

Check-In Schedule

Progress

- ☐ Application submitted
- ☐ Application submitted
- ☐ Application submitted
- ☐ Application submitted
- ☐ Interview
- ☐ Interview
- ☐ Interview

Implementation and Support

The client begins implementing the action plan, while the coach provides ongoing support and guidance. This includes regular check-ins, progress reviews, and adjustments to the plan as needed. The coach uses various techniques to motivate and hold the client accountable, such as offering feedback, celebrating successes, and addressing any challenges that arise.

Reflection and Adjustment

Periodically, the coach and client reflect on the progress made toward the goals. They assess what's working well and what might need to change. This reflective process helps in making necessary adjustments to the action plan and ensures that the client stays aligned with their overall objectives.

FACTORS THAT DETERMINE SUCCESS

Success is a multifaceted concept, shaped by a combination of personal qualities, habits, and external circumstances—many of which are beyond our control. While each person's path to success is unique, internal qualities such as mindset, discipline, resilience, and a commitment to continuous learning often play a crucial role in determining outcomes. As job coaches, we can encourage our clients to strengthen these internal qualities, thereby increasing their likelihood of achieving success in their chosen fields or other areas of life.

Internal Factors

- Goal Setting and Clear Vision
- Self-Discipline and Consistency
- Resilience and Perseverance
- Continuous Learning and Adaptability
- Strong Work Ethic and Discipline
- Emotional Intelligence
- Networking and Building Relationships
- Taking Calculated Risks
- Focus on Health and Wellbeing
- Gratitude and Giving Back
- Growth or Fixed Mindset
- Confidence
- Knowledge and Skills
- Time Management and Organizational Skills
- Networking and Relationships
- Values and Integrity (Ethical Behavior, Purpose and Meaning)

External Factors

- Environment and Opportunities
- Access to Resources
- Support System
- Luck and Timing
- Access to Education and Resources
- Socioeconomic Background (Family Wealth and Support)
- Quality of Education
- Financial Resources
- Geographical Location (Urban vs. Rural Opportunities, Proximity to Industry Hubs)
- Cultural and Societal Norms (Cultural Expectations, Discrimination and Bias)
- Economic Conditions (Local and Global Economy, Industry Trends)
- Government Policies and Regulations
- Access to Support Networks (Mentorship and Guidance, Professional Networks, Family and Community Support)
- Political and Social Climate

RESOURCES FOR JOB COACHES

- College Tours www.thecollegetour.com

- Dirty Jobs https://www.discovery.com/shows/dirty-jobs

Personality/Career Aptitude Assessments

- 16 Personalities www.16personalities.com
- My Next Move https://www.mynextmove.org
- ONet Interest Profiler https://www.mynextmove.org/explore/ip

- My Skills My Future https://www.myskillsmyfuture.org/
- The Clifton Strengths Assessment

https://www.gallup.com/cliftonstrengths/en/253868/popular-cliftonstrengths-assessment-products.aspx

Entrepreneurship Resources

- US Small Business Administration – Find Small Business Development Centers

https://www.sba.gov/local-assistance/resource-partners/small-business-development-centers-sbdc

- Service Corps of Retired Executives (SCORE) https://www.score.org/

College Planning

...Conduct an online search for – *College Planning Assessments*

3

Resumes and Letters

- Principles of Effective Resume Writing
- Letters to the Employer
- Resources for Job Coaches

PRINCIPLES OF EFFECTIVE RESUME WRITING

A resume is a document that provides potential employers with a summary of a candidate's prior work experience, education, and accomplishments. Resumes serve as a key tool in the job application process. While some employers require a resume as part of the application, others may not. Regardless, having a well-written resume is important and often necessary for securing employment.

Tools for creating resumes

- MS Word has different Resume and Letter templates that make it easy to create resumes and letters
- Indeed - https://www.indeed.com/create-resume
- Books such as, "Expert Resumes" by Wendy Enelow and Louise Kursmar

Types of Resumes

Chronological Resumes focus on work history, with the most recent job listed first.

Functional Resumes focus on experience and skills. This format is a good choice if there are gaps in employment.

Combined Resumes list skills and experience first, then work history in chronological order.

...Explain to your client what a Master Resume is.

Master Resume

A master resume is a comprehensive document that details an individual's work experience, education, skills, certifications, and accomplishments. It is a centralized resource that helps the job seeker create tailored resumes for specific job applications. Each resume should be customized to highlight the most relevant experiences and skills for the job the individual is applying for.

...We can have multiple resumes and should tailor each resume to the job.

The applicant should carefully review the job posting to identify key elements and frequently occurring keywords or phrases that highlight the employer's priorities and what they seek in a candidate. This includes the job title, required qualifications, essential skills, specific duties or responsibilities, and the company's mission, values, and culture. By aligning the resume with these elements, the applicant can demonstrate their suitability for the job, increasing their chances of being hired or selected for an interview.

Sample Job Posting

Job Title: Grocery Clerk

Location: ABC Supermarket, Anytown, USA

Job Type: Part-Time/Full-Time

Job Description: ABC Supermarket is seeking a friendly and reliable Grocery Clerk to join our team. The ideal candidate will be responsible for maintaining a well-stocked and organized store, providing exceptional customer service, and ensuring a clean and safe shopping environment.

Key Responsibilities:

- Stock shelves, displays, and coolers with products
- Rotate and check dates on perishable items
- Assist customers in locating products and answering questions
- Operate cash registers and handle transactions accurately
- +Maintain cleanliness of aisles, shelves, and storage areas
- Assist with inventory management and ordering supplies as needed

Qualifications:

- High school diploma or equivalent
- Prior retail or grocery store experience preferred
- Strong customer service skills
- Ability to lift up to 50 pounds and stand for extended periods
- Basic math skills for handling transactions
- Flexible schedule, including weekends and holidays

Benefits:

- Competitive pay
- Employee discounts
- Opportunities for advancement

- Friendly and supportive work environment

How to Apply: Interested candidates should submit their resume and a brief cover letter outlining their relevant experience and availability to [email@example.com].

Elements of a Resume

Full Name of Job Seeker
Personal/Contact Information
Address, telephone number, email
LinkedIn link or ePortfolio web address (optional)

Objective
The Objective is the job title you are applying for.

Statement of Qualifications
In 2-3 sentences summarize your qualifications for the job you are applying for. The statement should be related to the specific position for which you are applying. Example: *Experienced customer service professional with a strong background in client relations and sales. Demonstrated ability to communicate effectively, resolve conflicts, and provide exceptional service. Committed to creating positive customer experiences and fostering long-term client loyalty.*

Education
School name, City and State, date of graduation, course highlights (courses directly related to the job or your career field and special abilities), certificates, diplomas, and degrees

Work and Related Experience
Jobs, internships, or volunteer work - Include position title, company/organization, city/state, dates and a brief list or description of the job duties.

Awards and Honors
Academic, musical, athletic and or other recognition. Include name of the award/honor, who awarded it, and when it was awarded.

Activities/Hobbies
Include your role in the position, the organization, and dates.
Example: Captain, Shorewood High School, Volley Ball Team, 1999 and 2001

Skills
Soft skills examples: Responsible, Self-Motivated, Hardworking, Energetic, Outgoing
Hard skills examples: Research and Writing, Computer Skills, Public Speaking, Bilingual, Current certifications: Licenses, permits, and credentials

Good Resume Tips

- Resumes should be 1-2 pages
- Easy to read
- Use Times New Roman or Arial font
- 1 to 1.5-inch margins
- The format should be consistent
- Avoid using acronyms
- Avoid exaggerating skills or experience
- Include a professional email
- You don't need to put your full address (city & state is sufficient)
- Do not include birth date, health status or social security number
- Do not include references or statements like, *"Will provide references upon request"*
- Use good quality/wrinkle-free paper if providing an employer a hard copy
- Always have someone proofread your resume

Email Examples

- partygirl@umail.com   *not professional
- Lily2020@umail.com
- LilyLovato@umail.com *most professional

LETTERS TO THE EMPLOYER

Each of these letters serves a specific purpose in the job search process, helping job seekers communicate effectively with potential employers and build strong professional relationships.

Letters of Interest

A *Cover Letter* accompanies an application or resume when applying for a specific job. It introduces the applicant, expresses interest in the position, and highlights relevant qualifications.

A *Letter of Interest*, on the other hand, is used to inquire about potential job opportunities, even when no specific openings are advertised. It showcases the applicant's skills, experience, and enthusiasm for the company, aiming to make a positive impression and potentially open doors to future opportunities.

The letter of interest should include an introduction explaining the purpose of writing and specifying the desired position. It should also provide a summary of relevant experience, skills, qualifications, and accomplishments. Additionally, it should conclude with a call to action, indicating the applicant's willingness to interview or discuss potential opportunities.

Thank You Letter

A *Thank You Letter* is sent by a job seeker to an employer after an interview to express gratitude for the opportunity, reaffirm interest in the position, and highlight relevant qualifications. It helps keep the candidate top-of-mind and demonstrates professionalism and courtesy.

The thank you letter should include an expression of gratitude for the interview, a brief recap of key qualifications and interest in the role, a mention of any follow-up actions or next steps, and a reaffirmation of enthusiasm for the position and company.

Reference Letters

A *Reference Letter* is written by a former employer, colleague, teacher, or other professional acquaintance who can attest to the job seeker's skills, experience, and character. It provides third-party validation of the candidate's qualifications and is often requested during the hiring process.

The *Reference Letter* should include confirmation of the job seeker's skills, experience, and character, specific examples or anecdotes illustrating their strengths, and a recommendation for the candidate to be considered for the position.

A *Letter of Recommendation* is similar but typically more formal and detailed. It is often requested for job applications, scholarships, or academic programs, offering a comprehensive endorsement of the candidate's abilities and potential.

The letter of recommendation should provide a detailed overview of the job seeker's skills, achievements, and character, Include specific examples demonstrating their strengths and accomplishments, and give a strong recommendation for the candidate to be selected for the role or program.

Statement of Qualifications

A *Statement of Qualifications* is a document requested by an employer as part of an application packet. It outlines the applicant's relevant skills, experiences, and qualifications that make them suitable for the position.

The goal is to present a compelling case for why the candidate is a good fit for the role, emphasizing their potential to contribute effectively to the organization's goals and objectives. The employer may provide specific instructions on writing and formatting the statement.

Diversity Statement

A *Diversity Statement* is requested by employers as part of an application packet to assess an applicant's understanding, commitment, and contributions to diversity, equity, and inclusion (DEI).

In this statement, applicants reflect on their experiences and perspectives related to diversity, describing how they have engaged with diverse groups and fostered inclusive environments in both personal and professional settings. This allows employers to evaluate how well the candidate's values and experiences align with the company's DEI goals and culture.

List of References

It is common for employers to ask applicants for a list of references. A *List of References* or *Resume References* is a document that provides contact information for individuals who can provide positive feedback about your abilities, performance, qualifications, work ethic, skills, and character. These references are typically people you have worked with in a professional or academic capacity. Having a well-prepared list of references can enhance your job application.

Choose references who are familiar with your work in a professional context, such as former managers, colleagues, clients, or professors. Avoid using family members or friends.

Always ask for permission before listing someone as a reference to ensure they are willing and prepared to speak on your behalf.

In a separate document from your resume and cover letter, in a clear and organized manner, use the same or similar format than your resume (e.g., font and font size). Typically, 3-5 references are enough unless otherwise specified by the employer.

Key components for a List of References

Contact Information: Each reference should include the person's full name, job title, company or organization, phone number, and email address. Ensure the contact information is up-to-date and accurate.

Relationship Description: Provide a brief description of your relationship with each reference, such as how you know them and in what capacity you worked together (e.g., supervisor, coworker, professor).

Example:

Jane Smith
Senior Project Manager, XYZ Corporation
Phone: (123) 456-7890
Email: jane.smith@xyzcorp.com
Relationship: Former colleague

...Remind your client to keep all items, such as resources, sample letters, resumes etc., in a binder for future reference.

...Encourage your client to always ask someone to proofread documents they plan to submit to the employer (Resumes, cover letters, etc.)

RESOURCES FOR JOB COACHES

Resume Builders

- Cultivated Culture https://cultivatedculture.com/resume-templates/
- Teal https://www.tealhq.com/
- Resume.co https://resume.co/
- Resume Now https://www.resume-now.com/
- Resume Nerd https://www.resumenerd.com/
- My Perfect Resume https://www.myperfectresume.com/

Books

- *Expert Resumes for Career Changers* by Wendy Enelow and Louise Kursmark

...Conduct an internet search for samples or templates of resumes, cover letters, list of references, etc.

4

The Job Search

- Tailored Job Searches
- Finding Job Vacancies
- Other Job Search Techniques for Job Seekers
- Networking and Building Professional Connections
- Resources for Job Coaches

TAILORED JOB SEARCHES

Effective job search techniques are crucial for maximizing opportunities and securing the desired position. Tailor the job search to align with your client's needs and preferences.

The initial assessment with your client will help determine where and how they should look for job openings, as discussed in Chapter 2.

Key Elements

1. What type of jobs do they want to apply for?

2. Identify interests, strengths, skills, and areas for improvement.

3. What jobs are they qualified for? What experience and skills do they have?

4. Does the client have basic computer skills and access to a computer? Can they conduct online searches, send emails, type letters, submit applications online, etc.?

5. When do they have time to dedicate to their job search?

Knowing these things will let you and your client know where to start looking for job vacancies.

FINDING JOB VACANCIES

Online Job Boards

Ninety-nine percent of jobs require online applications, making basic computer skills and internet navigation essential.

LinkedIn and Indeed are popular platforms where job seekers across the U.S. can find employment opportunities. Additionally, each state has its state-specific job board. **Note, websites change over time.*

Alabama Works	https://alabamaworks.alabama.gov/
Alaska Job Center Network	https://jobs.alaska.gov/
Arizona Job Connection	https://www.azjobconnection.gov/
Arkansas JobLink	https://www.arjoblink.arkansas.gov/
California, CalJOBS	https://www.caljobs.ca.gov/vosnet/
Colorado. Connecting Colorado	https://www.connectingcolorado.com/
Connecticut CTHires	https://www.cthires.com/
Delaware Job Link	https://joblink.delaware.gov/
Florida, Employ Florida	https://www.employflorida.com/
Georgia, Worksource Georgia	https://www.worksourcegaportal.com/
Hawaii, Hire Net Hawaii	https://www.hirenethawaii.com/
Idaho Works	https://idahoworks.gov/
Illinois Job Link	https://illinoisjoblink.illinois.gov/
Indiana Career Connect	https://www.indianacareerconnect.com/
Iowa Workforce Development	https://workforce.iowa.gov/
Kansas Works	https://www.kansasworks.com/

Kentucky Career Center	https://kcc.ky.gov/
Louisiana Workforce Commission	https://www.laworks.net/
Maine Job Link	https://joblink.maine.gov/
Maryland: Maryland Workforce Exchange	https://mwejobs.maryland.gov/
Massachusetts: MassHire JobQuest	https://jobquest.dcs.eol.mass.gov/
Michigan: Pure Michigan Talent Connect	https://www.mitalent.org/
Minnesota Works	https://www.minnesotaworks.net/
Mississippi Works	https://mississippiworks.org/
Missouri Job Center	https://jobs.mo.gov/
Montana: MontanaWorks	https://montanaworks.gov/
Nebraska: NEworks	https://neworks.nebraska.gov/
Nevada: EmployNV	https://www.employnv.gov/
New Hampshire: NHWorks Job Match System	https://nhworksjobmatch.nhes.nh.gov/
New Jersey: NJ.gov Jobs	https://www.nj.gov/nj/employ/
New Mexico Workforce Connection	https://www.jobs.state.nm.us
New York: NYS Job Bank	https://newyork.usnlx.com/
North Carolina: NCWorks Online	https://www.ncworks.gov/
North Dakota: Job Service North Dakota	https://www.jobsnd.com/
Ohio: OhioMeansJobs	https://ohiomeansjobs.ohio.gov/
Oklahoma: OKJobMatch	https://okjobmatch.com/
Oregon: WorkSource Oregon	https://www.worksourceoregon.org/
Pennsylvania: PA CareerLink	https://www.pacareerlink.pa.gov/jponline/
Rhode Island: EmployRI	https://www.employri.org/
South Carolina: SC Works Online Services	https://jobs.scworks.org/
South Dakota: South Dakota Works	https://www.southdakotaworks.org/
Tennessee: Jobs4TN	https://www.tn.gov/jobs4tn
Texas: WorkInTexas	https://www.workintexas.com/
Utah: jobs.utah.gov	https://jobs.utah.gov/
Vermont: Vermont JobLink	https://vermontjoblink.com/
Virginia: Virginia Workforce Connection	https://vawc.virginia.gov/
Washington: WorkSource Washington	https://www.worksourcewa.com/
West Virginia: Workforce West Virginia	https://workforcewv.org/
Wisconsin: Job Center of Wisconsin	https://jobcenterofwisconsin.com/
Wyoming: Wyoming at Work	https://hire.wyo.gov/

There are also industry specific websites, for example:

Government Jobs	https://www.governmentjobs.com/
Hospitality Jobs	https://poachedjobs.com/
For Justice Impacted	https://www.honestjobs.com/
Nonprofit Jobs	https://www.idealist.org/
Jobs in Entertainment	https://www.mandy.com/

...Some websites allow you to set up alerts that notify you when there's new listings.

...You and your client may come across jobs they don't quite qualify for yet. They should save the job ads in a folder labeled "Future Jobs."

Company Websites / Social Media

Most businesses have a link on their website where job seekers can apply directly for open positions. Job seekers should regularly check the careers section of the websites of companies they are interested in working for.

Following companies and industry leaders on social media platforms can also be a good way to stay updated on job openings and industry trends.

OTHER JOB SEARCH TECHNIQUES FOR JOB SEEKERS

Cold Calling Employers

Call the business you want to work for and inquire whether they are hiring and where to go to apply.

Utilize Local Career Centers

Find local job centers on https://www.careeronestop.org/ and search by zip code.

Services vary at each job center. Local job centers may offer 1:1 assistance for job seekers and specialized populations, job leads, job fairs, workshops/webinars, and funding for job training.

Professional Organizations and Associations

Many industries have professional associations, some of which feature job boards on their websites. Some of their websites don't require membership to view job postings.

Tell People

Inform your social network (whether acquaintances from school, neighbors, family, or friends) that you are seeking new employment opportunities.

College Career Services

College career centers may offer resume reviews, mock interviews, and job search workshops. Former college students can also leverage college alumni networks for job leads and mentorship.

Utilize Recruitment and Staffing Agencies

Sign up with temporary agencies, recruitment firms, or staffing agencies that specialize in your industry to gain access to job opportunities not publicly advertised.

Working for temporary staffing agencies is a great way to gain experience and skills and make connections. Temporary positions can also lead to permanent employment.

Apprenticeships

An apprenticeship is a structured training program that blends paid, on-the-job experience with formal classroom instruction. This hands-on approach enables participants to develop the specific skills needed for a trade or profession, all while earning an income. Upon completion, it often leads to certification or qualification.

Apprenticeships are available in a wide range of fields, including:

- Skilled Trades: Electricians, Plumbers, Carpenters, Welders, HVAC Technicians
- Healthcare: Medical Coders, Dental Assistants, Surgical Technologists, Pharmacy Technicians
- Technology and IT: Software Developers, Cybersecurity Analysts, Network Administrators, Data Analysts
- Manufacturing: CNC Machinists, Production Technicians, Industrial Maintenance Workers
- Hospitality and Culinary Arts: Chefs, Bakers, Hospitality Managers

- Transportation and Logistics: Commercial Drivers, Warehouse Technicians, Logistics Coordinators
- Business and Finance: Accountants, Project Managers, Insurance Underwriters

Participating in an apprenticeship program can provide job seekers with numerous advantages, such as:

- Hands-on Experience: Apprentices gain real-world training directly related to their career path, enhancing job readiness.
- Earnings While Learning: Apprenticeships allow participants to earn a salary while developing skills, helping to reduce the need for student loans.
- Industry-Recognized Credentials: Upon completion, apprentices receive certifications or qualifications that are often recognized across the industry.
- Job Placement Opportunities: Many apprenticeships lead directly to full-time employment with the sponsoring employer.
- Networking: Apprentices connect with professionals in their field, creating doors for future opportunities.
- Increased Job Security: With practical experience and credentials, apprentices are often more competitive and enjoy greater job security.

Apprenticeship programs can be found on labor and employment websites, through local community colleges and trade schools, industry associations, unions, company websites, job boards, networking, and workforce development centers. As apprenticeships can be competitive, it's beneficial to prepare a polished resume, emphasize relevant skills or experience, and ensure all specific requirements are met before applying.

Application Process for Apprenticeships

- Research and Choose Programs: Identify apprenticeship programs that align with your career interests and review their specific requirements and timelines.
- Prepare Application Materials: Typical applications require a resume, cover letter, and sometimes a high school diploma or GED. Some programs may also request transcripts, letters of recommendation, or a statement of interest.
- Complete the Application Form: Application processes vary; some programs use online forms, while others may require in-person submissions at local training centers.
- Testing and Interviews: Some apprenticeships require pre-assessment tests (e.g., basic math or mechanical aptitude), followed by an interview to evaluate motivation and suitability.
- Meet Eligibility Requirements: Some programs have specific eligibility criteria, such as age (typically 18+), residency, or prior coursework or experience.
- Acceptance and Enrollment: If accepted, you'll typically receive onboarding information, which may include orientation, schedule, pay details, and required coursework.

NETWORKING AND BUILDING PROFESSIONAL CONNECTIONS

Professional Branding

Enhance Your LinkedIn Profile: Craft a compelling headline, upload a professional photo, and provide a detailed summary of your skills, experience, and achievements to attract attention from potential employers.

Create a Personal Website or Online Portfolio (ePortfolio): Build an online portfolio to showcase your work, particularly if you're in a creative field, allowing potential employers or clients to easily view your accomplishments.

Leverage Professional Networks

Leverage both online and in-person professional networks to connect with industry professionals, join relevant groups, and actively participate in discussions.

Attend Events

Attend job fairs, industry conferences, webinars, and networking events to connect with potential employers and discover job openings.

Informational Interviews

Request informational interviews with professionals in your target industry to gain valuable insights and build meaningful connections.

Leverage Social Media

Social media platforms provide opportunities to share industry-relevant content and engage with professionals in similar fields, increasing visibility. Online communities are also excellent for building professional connections by exchanging resources and learning about job opportunities.

Potential Partnerships for Job Coaches

- Other job centers, career counselors, and job coaches
- State and county workforce or economic development departments
- Local trade schools, colleges, and universities
- Employers, industry leaders, and human resources professionals
- Local Chambers of Commerce
- Apprenticeship programs
- Labor trade unions and associations
- Business centers
- Women's business centers
- Local libraries
- Local churches
- Local nonprofits and resource centers

RESOURCES FOR JOB COACHES

Job Boards

- Indeed https://indeed.com/
- Flex Jobs https://www.flexjobs.com/

Connecting with Others

- LinkedIn https://www.linkedin.com/
- Hive Index https://thehiveindex.com/

Faith-based

- Christian Jobs https://www.christianjobs.com/
- Ministry Jobs https://ministryjobs.com/
- Church Jobs Online https://www.churchjobsonline.com/
- Church Staffing https://www.churchstaffing.com/

Locate local job centers

- Career Onestop https://www.careeronestop.org/

...Conduct an online search for your state's workforce development job board.

5

The Application Process

- Preparing Application Materials
- Resources for Job Coaches

PREPARING APPLICATION MATERIALS

Once a strong resume is created and job seekers have the job-ready essentials, they can begin applying for jobs. Job postings typically outline the application process.

The application process for every job opening can vary. Some may be quick and straightforward, while others could take over a year to complete. Job seekers should be prepared to dedicate time to this process. Using platforms like Indeed can make applying fast and easy. Some applications may only take a minute to submit, while others could take 30 minutes or more. Additionally, some applications may require assessments.

...After applying, it could take months before hearing back from the employer. Employers may respond via phone, email, or letter. Responses could include a denial letter, or in some cases, no communication at all. Explain to your client that some employers use Applicant Tracking Systems (ATS). Therefore, it is important to use keywords from the job posting on their applications and resumes.

The Master Application

A *Master Application* includes all the information typically required on a job application, such as personal details, employment history, educational background, references, and other relevant information. Considered a living document, the master application is designed for job seekers to use when completing other applications. It allows individuals to easily access all necessary information in one place, ensuring both accuracy and consistency.

...Explain to your client what a Master Application is. As we continue to work in new jobs or participate in some type of work or volunteer experience, gain new skills, or earn certifications, we continuously update information to our Master Application.

Background Checks

Many employers require background checks as part of the application process to assess the suitability and reliability of potential employees. These checks typically involve verifying an applicant's identity, employment history, educational qualifications, and criminal record. Depending on the nature of the job, employers may also review credit reports, driving records, and social media activity. Background checks help employers mitigate risks by confirming the accuracy of the information provided and identifying potential red flags that could affect job performance or workplace safety. By conducting thorough checks, employers aim to protect their business, employees, and customers while fostering a secure and trustworthy work environment.

Exams

Some employers require exams as part of the application process to assess candidates' skills, knowledge, and suitability for specific roles. These exams can range from general aptitude tests, which measure logical reasoning, numerical ability, and verbal skills, to job-specific assessments that evaluate technical skills or industry knowledge relevant to the position. Additionally, personality tests may be used to assess a candidate's fit with the company culture and team dynamics.

Some employers require candidates to pass an exam before submitting their application for a vacancy. Others may require the submission of the application first, and if the employer is interested in the applicant, they will invite them to take the exam.

Many government jobs require candidates to pass exams, which may take place either in person or online.

There are many books and online resources designed specifically to help individuals prepare for exams in a wide variety of subjects and career fields. Some websites offer free and paid materials such as practice tests, study guides, and flashcards. Similarly, major book retailers and libraries carry exam prep books that help users review content, understand test formats, and build test-taking strategies. These tools can be especially useful for certifications, standardized tests, and professional licensing exams.

Organization

Being organized with hard copy documents or computer files is crucial for job and career development, as it allows us to access the necessary items when we need them. We should encourage our clients to use file folders or binders and create separate folders on their computers to store documents they've used in the past. Saving these materials will be helpful for them in the future.

...As job seekers create resumes and cover letters, they should save them on their computer and name them for future use as templates. When they come across job leads, they should either print them out or note them down. As they gain experience, skills, etc., they should update their Master Application and Master Resume. As job seekers apply for jobs, they should track the dates they applied and set reminders on their calendars to follow up.

RESOURCES FOR JOB COACHES

Job Applications

- Simplify https://simplify.jobs/
- Applyish https://applyish.com/
- Careerflow.ai https://www.careerflow.ai/

6

Interviewing

- Preparing to Answer Interview Questions
- Gaps in Employment
- Preparing Clients for Job Interviews
- Confidence, Interview Etiquette, and Body Language
- Interview Attire
- Virtual Interviews
- Alleviating Anxiety
- Resources for Job Seekers

The purpose of a job interview is to allow both the employer and the candidate to assess whether there is a good fit between the role and the applicant. From the employer's perspective, it provides an opportunity to evaluate the candidate's skills, experience, and qualifications in a more dynamic setting than a resume alone can offer. For the candidate, the interview is a chance to showcase their abilities, discuss past accomplishments, and demonstrate how they can contribute to the company's success. It also provides the candidate with a better understanding of the role, the team, and the company culture.

PREPARING TO ANSWER INTERVIEW QUESTIONS

Company Research and Role Familiarization

Coaches can guide clients in researching the company's mission, values, and recent news, as well as thoroughly reviewing the job description. This preparation enables the client to ask insightful questions and demonstrate genuine interest in both the role and the company.

Since it's impossible to predict exactly which questions the employer will ask during the interview, advise your clients to take time to review common interview questions and write down their responses as they would want to answer them during the interview.

Commonly Asked Questions

- *Tell me about yourself?*
- *Why do want this job?*
- *What are your greatest strengths?*
- *What are your weaknesses?*
- *Tell us about a time you had a challenge and how did you deal with it?*
- *Tell us about a time you exercised leadership?*
- *Tell us about a time when you had a conflict or disagreement with another employee and how did you handle it?*

- *Why are you the best candidate for this position?*

How should we answer the question, *"Tell me about yourself?"*

When answering the question, "Tell me about yourself," it's important to provide a concise, well-structured response that highlights your professional background and aligns with the role you're applying for. This approach ensures your answer is focused, professional, and tailored to the job, giving the interviewer a clear sense of who you are and how you can contribute to their organization.

Start with Your Professional Background

Start by summarizing your career path, focusing on the roles most relevant to the position you're applying for. Highlight your current or most recent role, key responsibilities, and any achievements that showcase your qualifications.

Example: *"I'm currently a marketing manager at XYZ Company, where I lead a team responsible for managing digital campaigns for our top clients. Over the past three years, I've successfully increased client engagement by 20% through innovative strategies."*

Highlight Key Skills and Strengths

Highlight skills or strengths that make you a strong candidate, tailored to the job description. Emphasize how your experience can benefit the company.

Example: *"I have a strong background in data analysis and campaign optimization, enabling me to make data-driven decisions that enhance campaign performance."*

Connect Your Experience to the Role

Conclude by explaining why you're excited about the opportunity and how your experience aligns with the company's needs. This demonstrates your research and genuine interest in the position.

Example: *"I'm excited about the opportunity at ABC Company because my experience in driving digital growth aligns with the innovative projects your team is pursuing. I'm eager to contribute and help elevate your campaigns."*

The STAR Method

The *STAR Method* is an effective way to answer interview questions by organizing your experiences into four components: Situation, Task, Action, and Result. Teaching your clients this method can help them communicate their experiences clearly and effectively.

Situation: Start by describing the context and details of the scenario.

Task: Outline your specific responsibilities in that situation.

Action: Walk through the actions you took to address the challenge.

Result: Conclude by highlighting the outcomes of your actions.

You can spot STAR-based questions with prompts like:

> *"Tell me about a time when ..."*
> *"What do you do when ..."*
> *"Have you ever ..."*
> *"Give me an example of ..."*
> *"Describe a situation ..."*

For example, if an interviewer asks, *"Tell me about a time when you had to be very strategic in order to meet all of your top priorities,"* you could respond like this:

Situation: *"In my previous sales role, I was responsible for transitioning our team to a new customer relationship management (CRM) system while also maintaining my daily sales responsibilities."*

Task: *"My goal was to complete the CRM migration by the start of Quarter 3 without letting my sales performance fall below target."*

Action: *"To achieve this, I managed my time carefully, dedicating an hour each day exclusively to the CRM transition. This included transferring data, cleaning outdated contacts, and updating information. By doing this, I made consistent progress on the project while staying on top of my regular tasks."*

Result: *"The migration was completed two weeks ahead of schedule, and I finished the quarter 10% above my sales goals. Additionally, the new CRM system enhanced our team's organization, leading to a 25% increase in department sales year-over-year."*

Mock Interviews

Conducting practice interviews allows clients to simulate the real experience. A job coach can ask common interview questions and provide feedback on responses, body language, and overall presentation. Mock interviews help clients refine their answers and enhance their ability to think on their feet.

By preparing thoroughly for mock interviews, job coaches can provide valuable, realistic practice that boosts clients' confidence and improves their interviewing skills.

Steps for Conducting Mock Interviews

1. Familiarize Yourself with the Client's Background: Review the client's resume, career goals, and the specific job description they are preparing for.

2. Prepare Relevant Interview Questions: Create a list of questions commonly asked in the industry and specific to the job the client is applying for. Refer to the job advertisement to craft questions related to the responsibilities or required skills. Include behavioral interview questions to evaluate the client's past experiences and problem-solving abilities.

3. Set Up a Realistic Interview Environment: Choose a quiet, professional setting that simulates an actual interview atmosphere.

4. Role-Play as the Interviewer: Assume the role of the interviewer with a formal demeanor to create an authentic experience.

5. Explain the Process: Inform the client about what to expect, including the types of questions and the duration of the interview.

6. Encourage Professionalism: Advise the client to approach the mock interview seriously and provide guidelines for effective responses.

7. Conduct the Mock Interview: Ask the prepared questions while observing the client's responses.

8. Take Detailed Notes: Document the client's answers, body language, and overall presentation to provide thorough feedback.

9. Provide Constructive Feedback: After the interview, offer honest feedback that highlights strengths and areas for improvement. Use specific examples from the mock interview to clarify your points and suggest practical enhancements.

10. Practice Through Repetition: Conduct multiple mock interviews if needed, allowing the client to practice and refine their responses.

11. Encourage Self-Assessment: Prompt the client to reflect on their performance and identify areas they believe need improvement.

12. Share Additional Resources: Provide the client with supplementary materials, such as articles, videos, or workshops, to support continuous improvement.

GAPS IN EMPLOYMENT

People experience employment gaps for various reasons and addressing them in a job interview requires a strategic approach. Common causes include personal or family matters, pursuing further education, health challenges, caregiving responsibilities, incarceration, or taking time off to travel. In some cases, gaps result from job loss due to economic downturns, company restructuring, or layoffs. Regardless of the reason, it's essential for job seekers to be prepared to discuss these periods openly and professionally during an interview.

Tips for Job Seekers

When discussing employment gaps, honesty is essential. Start by briefly acknowledging the gap and providing a concise explanation without too much detail. If the gap was due to personal reasons, such as health or caregiving, you can simply mention that you took time off to focus on family or a personal matter but are now ready and eager to return to work. If the gap involved pursuing education or skill development, highlight how you used that time to enhance your qualifications for the role. Focus on framing your response positively.

Another key aspect is to emphasize what you learned or accomplished during the gap. Whether you took on freelance projects, volunteered, or earned relevant certifications, showcasing how you used your time productively can help bridge the gap and demonstrate your commitment to personal growth. Employers appreciate candidates who remain proactive, even during periods of unemployment.

Finally, always steer the conversation back to your enthusiasm for the position and how your skills and experiences align with the job. By keeping the focus on what you can offer the company and maintaining a positive outlook, you can confidently and professionally address employment gap discussions.

For tips on discussing criminal history with an employer, see Chapter 10.

Template for Discussing Gaps in Employment

Provide a brief explanation for the employment gap, keeping the description concise and straightforward.

If addressing criminal charges, briefly explain the situation, express remorse and responsibility, highlight positive changes, and emphasize personal growth.

Reason for Gaps in Employment

____

____

Education Acquired

____

____

Employment History

____

____

New Skills Gained

____

____

Relevant Skills

____

____

Participation in Community Service

____

____

Character and Capabilities

____

____

Positive changes you have made in your life since the gap or incident

____

____

Rehabilitation programs, therapy, or counseling (optional)

____

____

Future goals/plans

____

____

PREPARING CLIENTS FOR JOB INTERVIEWS

A job coach can help clients prepare for interviews using practical strategies designed to boost their confidence, communication skills, and overall readiness.

Here are some best practices to teach job seekers.

Preparation

Once you receive and accept an interview offer, start researching the company. Understand its mission, values, products or services, and recent news. Familiarize yourself with the job description and how your skills align.

Confirm the interview format (in-person, phone, or video), time, location, and the names and roles of the interviewers.

Interview Settings

It's important to inform your clients that employers conduct interviews in various ways and settings. Interviews can be in-person, over the phone, or in a virtual space. They can range from casual to formal and may involve a single interviewer or a panel of 2 to 10 people. The length of interviews can also vary—some may last 10 minutes with only three questions, while others may involve 10 questions and take over an hour.

Interviews typically have four stages:

Introduction: The employer introduces themselves, provides information on the position, and may explain the interview format, including the number of questions to be asked.

Questioning: The employer asks the prepared questions.

Candidate's Questions: The interviewee is allowed to ask the employer or panel questions about the job.

Closing: The employer concludes the interview.

After an interview, some positions may require a second interview. Additionally, candidates might need to take a test before or after the interview as part of the selection process.

...The more an interviewer prepares, the better they will do.

CONFIDENCE, INTERVIEW ETIQUETTE, AND BODY LANGUAGE

Good interview etiquette is essential to making a positive impression on potential employers. Below are some best practices for before, during, and after an interview.

Tips for the Day Before the Interview

- Have your complete interview outfit ironed, and ready.
- Have necessary items ready – ID, folder, pen, paperwork, documents, forms, resume, references, letters of recommendation, etc.
- Map the interview location.
- Study for the interview and practice answering common interview questions.
- Go to sleep early to be well-rested.
- Write a thank you letter dated the day of the interview.

The Day of the Interview

- Prepare to speak clearly by practicing tongue twisters if needed.
- For in-person interviews, aim to arrive at least 15 minutes early. For virtual interviews, log in a few minutes in advance to check your technology.
- Upon arrival, silence your cell phone or set it to silent mode.

Professional Appearance

- Dress appropriately by wearing professional attire that matches the company culture. When in doubt, choose more formal clothing.
- Ensure you are well-groomed and presentable.

Confidence and Stress Management Techniques

Encourage your client to use stress management techniques, such as deep breathing, visualization, and positive affirmations, to help clients manage interview anxiety. These methods can help them stay calm and focused during the interview.

Polite and Courteous Behavior

Smile and greet everyone politely, from the receptionist to the interviewers. Use a firm handshake and maintain eye contact when greeting. Remember to say "please" and "thank you" as appropriate and avoid interrupting the interviewer.

Body Language

Relax but sit up straight to maintain good posture. Make eye contact to show confidence and engagement but avoid staring. Use natural hand gestures and minimize fidgeting.

Effective Communication

Maintain eye contact with your interviewers. Speak clearly and concisely, avoiding filler words like "um," "like," and "you know." Listen carefully to questions and comments, nodding to show understanding. Wait for the interviewer to finish speaking before responding. Take a moment to think before answering to ensure your responses are thoughtful and relevant.

Show Enthusiasm and Interest

Display enthusiasm for the role *and* the company. Smile and show genuine interest in the conversation. Prepare insightful questions about the company, team, and role to demonstrate your engagement.

Highlight Skills and Experiences

Use specific examples from your past experiences to showcase your skills and achievements. Utilize the STAR Method (Situation, Task, Action, Result) to structure your responses to behavioral questions.

Handling Difficult Questions

Stay calm and composed when faced with challenging questions. If you don't know the answer, it's better to admit it and express a willingness to learn rather than provide incorrect information.

Closing the Interview

Thank each interviewer for their time and express your continued interest in the role. Ask about the next steps in the hiring process and the expected timeline for a decision.

Follow-Up

Send a thank-you email or letter within 24 hours of the interview. Mention specific points from the conversation and reiterate your interest in the position.

INTERVIEW ATTIRE

Best practices for interview attire vary based on the industry, company culture, and job level, but there are general guidelines to make a professional impression. Tailor your attire to the company's dress code. For example, a startup might expect business casual, while a corporate law firm would require formal business attire. Dressing appropriately shows respect for the interview process and helps create a strong first impression.

For Men

Suit and Tie (Traditional Professional Settings): In formal industries like finance, law, or corporate roles, a classic dark suit (navy, black, or charcoal) with a tie is standard. Ensure the suit is well-fitted, pressed, and comfortable. Avoid clothing that is too tight, too loose, or distracting.

Shirt: Opt for a solid white or light-colored dress shirt that complements the suit.

Shoes: Wear polished, leather dress shoes (black or brown) with matching socks.

Accessories: Keep accessories simple and professional—minimal jewelry, a conservative tie, and a leather belt that matches your shoes.

Business Casual (Less Formal Settings): In industries like tech or creative fields, business casual might be more appropriate. This includes dress slacks or chinos paired with a button-down shirt or a blazer, without the need for a tie.

Hygiene and Grooming: Pay attention to personal hygiene. This includes clean, pressed clothes, well-groomed hair, and minimal fragrances. Ensure that facial hair is neatly trimmed, and hair is styled appropriately for a professional setting.

For Women

Tailored Suit or Professional Dress (Traditional Professional Settings)

For formal environments, a well-fitted pantsuit, skirt suit, or conservative dress is ideal. Neutral colors like black, navy, or gray are recommended. Ensure your clothing is comfortable and well-fitted, avoiding anything too tight, loose, or distracting.

Blouse or Top: Choose a solid color or subtle pattern that complements the suit. Avoid overly bold or revealing styles.

Shoes: Closed-toe pumps or flats in neutral tones (black, nude, or navy) are recommended. Heels should be moderate in height.

Accessories: Keep jewelry minimal and professional—small earrings, a simple necklace, and a watch are appropriate. Avoid large, distracting accessories.

Hygiene, Grooming, and Makeup: Pay attention to personal hygiene, including clean, pressed clothes and well-groomed hair. Use minimal fragrances. Keep makeup natural and avoid overly bright colors. Hair should be neatly styled and not distracting.

Business Casual (Less Formal Settings): For more relaxed environments, tailored slacks, skirts, or dresses paired with blouses or sweaters are suitable. A blazer can add a polished touch without requiring a full suit.

Flats or low-heeled closed-toe shoes are appropriate. Ensure shoes are clean and polished.

VIRTUAL INTERVIEWS

Interviewing for a job virtually requires a different set of best practices to ensure that a strong and professional impression is made. Here are some best practices to teach clients.

Check Technology

Before the interview, ensure your internet connection is stable, and test your microphone, camera, and any required software (e.g., Zoom, Teams). Confirm that everything works smoothly to avoid technical issues during the interview.

Professional Setting

Choose a quiet, well-lit space free from distractions. Your background should be clean and organized. If possible, position yourself facing natural light to ensure you are clearly visible on camera.

Minimize Distractions

Keep pets, phones, and other distractions away from your interview space. Close unnecessary tabs or applications on your computer to maintain focus and avoid interruptions.

Prepare and Practice

Just as you would for an in-person interview, prepare to answer common interview questions, research the company, and practice your responses. This ensures you come across as polished and well-prepared.

Dress Professionally

Even for a virtual interview, dress as if attending in person. Professional attire helps you make a positive impression and can boost your confidence.

Maintain Good Eye Contact

During the virtual interview, look directly into the camera when speaking to create the illusion of eye contact. This builds rapport with the interviewer. Avoid watching yourself on the screen or frequently looking down at notes.

Alleviating Anxiety

It's normal to feel nervous during interviews. High levels of anxiety can impact performance, so proper preparation is crucial.

Studies show that a significant majority of people experience interview anxiety. According to a JDP survey, 93% of candidates reported feeling anxious about their interviews.

Source: JDP. (2020, January 29). How Americans prepare for interviews. https://www.jdp.com/blog/how-to-prepare-for-interviews-2020/

Job coaches can teach relaxation and confidence-boosting techniques to help clients reduce nervousness and build confidence before and during job interviews.

Deep Breathing Exercises

Practice controlled breathing by inhaling deeply through the nose and exhaling slowly through the mouth. This calms the nervous system and reduces anxiety.

Progressive Muscle Relaxation (PMR)

This technique involves tensing and then relaxing different muscle groups. Focusing on relaxation helps relieve tension and promotes a sense of calm.

Visualization

Candidates can visualize themselves succeeding in the interview by imagining a positive outcome. This mental rehearsal technique reduces anxiety and boosts self-confidence.

Mindfulness

Practicing mindfulness involves focusing on the present moment without judgment. This technique helps reduce pre-interview stress by keeping attention on the present instead of worrying about the future.

Positive Affirmations

Repeating positive affirmations can build confidence and counteract negative thoughts. Phrases like *"I am prepared"* or *"I can handle this interview"* reinforce a sense of capability and calmness.

...As you Job Coach others, you will also benefit in your own career journey. You will inevitably improve in your own job-readiness skills, and seek new employment opportunities.

RESOURCES FOR JOB COACHES

Interview preparation websites

- Interviewsby.ai https://www.interviewsby.ai/
- Talk Hiring https://www.talkhiring.com/mockinterview
- aiApply https://aiapply.co/
- Yoodli https://yoodli.ai/

...Conduct an internet search for interviewing tips or commonly asked questions.

7

Coaching Youth

- Work Permits for Minors
- Understanding the Developmental Needs of Youth
- Strategies and Techniques
- Workshops and Webinars for Groups
- Partner with Parents
- Studies on Youth Employment
- Resources for Job Coaches

WORK PERMITS FOR MINORS

In the U.S., federal law allows minors to begin working at age 14, though some states have stricter age requirements. Many states require minors under 18 to obtain a work permit or age certificate, typically through their school or state labor department. While requirements vary by state, they usually include:

- Parental/Guardian Consent
- Proof of Age (e.g., birth certificate or other official documentation)
- Employer Commitment (Some states require employers to sign a form confirming compliance with youth labor laws)

For jobs involving more physical or hazardous tasks, the minimum age may be 16 or 18, depending on the role and industry. Minors under 18 are generally prohibited from working in hazardous occupations, such as operating heavy machinery, manufacturing, or construction.

Some states or specific circumstances may exempt minors from permit requirements for jobs like babysitting, household chores, or working in family-owned businesses, provided these roles do not involve hazardous tasks.

For detailed federal guidelines and state-specific requirements, visit the U.S. Department of Labor's Youth Employment Information page.

Source: U.S. Department of Labor. Youth & Young Worker Employment. November 22, 2024. Retrieved from https://www.dol.gov/general/topic/youthlabor

UNDERSTANDING THE DEVELOPMENTAL NEEDS OF YOUTH

The term "youth" generally refers to individuals in the transitional phase between childhood and adulthood. The specific age range varies depending on the context and the organization defining it. However, youth are commonly considered to be between 15 and 24 years old.

When coaching youth in the workplace, it's important to recognize their unique needs, preferences, and developmental stages. Young individuals may be at different points in their personal and professional growth, so coaching approaches should be tailored accordingly.

Positive Youth Development

A collaboration of 22 federal departments and agencies that support youth has developed the following definition of Positive Youth Development (PYD):

"PYD is an intentional, prosocial approach that engages youth within their communities, schools, organizations, peer groups, and families in a productive and constructive manner. It recognizes, utilizes, and enhances young people's strengths while promoting positive outcomes by providing opportunities, fostering supportive relationships, and equipping youth with the necessary resources to develop their leadership skills."

Source: "Positive Youth Development." Youth.gov, U.S. Government, Nov. 22, 2024. https://youth.gov/youth-topics/positive-youth-development

The 6 Core Components (6 C's) of the Positive Youth Development (PYD) framework represent key outcomes for youth development:

Competence – A positive view of one's abilities in social, academic, cognitive, and vocational areas. It involves having the necessary skills to effectively navigate different aspects of life.

Confidence – A belief in one's ability to succeed and make a difference. This reflects an internal sense of self-worth and self-efficacy.

Connection – A sense of belonging and being part of a supportive network. This includes strong bonds with family, peers, schools, and the community.

Character – A commitment to principles and values that guide behavior. This includes integrity, morality, and respect for societal and cultural norms.

Caring/Compassion – The ability to understand and share the feelings of others. This fosters empathy, prosocial behavior, and a commitment to supporting others' well-being.

When these five C's are nurtured, they lead to a sixth C – Contribution.

Contribution – The active and positive involvement of young people in their communities and society. As youth develop their skills and attributes, they use them to give back and make a meaningful impact.

A job coach plays a crucial role in fostering these components.

- They enhance *Competence* by teaching essential job skills and helping youth navigate the work environment.
- They build *Confidence* by reinforcing self-assurance in abilities and career prospects.
- Through consistent interactions, they cultivate *Connection*, helping young people form positive workplace and community relationships.
- They instill *Character* by promoting ethical behavior and responsibility in a professional setting.
- They encourage *Caring/Compassion* by modeling empathy and teamwork.
- Ultimately, these combined efforts empower youth to *Contribute* meaningfully to their workplaces and communities, using their skills and values to create a lasting, positive impact.

...Teaching youth essential life skills can help prevent social problems (e.g., financial problems, job loss, homelessness) as they transition into adulthood.

STRATEGIES AND TECHNIQUES

By applying these techniques, job coaches can effectively support and empower youth in their career exploration and transition into the workforce.

Building Rapport and Trust

Establishing a supportive and trusting relationship is essential. Creating a safe space allows youth to openly express their concerns, goals, and aspirations, fostering confidence in the coaching process.

Addressing Barriers and Challenges

When providing job development assistance, be mindful of potential challenges youth may face, such as a lack of experience, transportation, or financial limitations, or family responsibilities. Offer guidance and connect them with resources to help overcome these barriers.

Resource Topics

- Career Exploration Websites
- Job Search Platforms
- Job Leads
- Youth-Focused Employment Programs
- Community Resources

Clarifying Interests and Goals

Help youth identify their interests, strengths, and career aspirations through exploration activities, assessments, and self-reflection exercises.

Some youth may already have a clear vision of their career goals, whether in work, college, or a specific profession. Others may need guidance and support in exploring different career paths and opportunities. Tailoring your approach to each individual's needs ensures they receive the right level of assistance in their career development journey.

Assessments and goal setting are discussed in Chapter 2.

Encourage clients to identify the "why" behind the goals they set. Understanding their motivations provides the drive and perseverance to overcome challenges and achieve their objectives.

Supporting Career Decision-Making

Guide youth in evaluating their options, considering the pros and cons of different career paths, and making well-informed decisions about their future.

Encouraging Independence and Self-Advocacy

Empower youth to take ownership of their career journey by fostering independence, self-advocacy, and decision-making skills.

Encouraging Volunteerism and Civic Engagement

Introduce youth to the concepts related to civic engagement and the benefits of volunteering or participating in community-based opportunities. These experiences can help build skills, expand networks, and enhance resumes.

Skill Development

Provide resources and guidance to help youth develop essential employability skills such as communication, teamwork, problem-solving, and time management.

Dual Enrollment

Explain the advantages of dual enrollment (or concurrent enrollment), which allows high school students to take college courses and earn college credits early, giving them a head start on their postsecondary education.

...Job coaches can assist their clients in finding opportunities and understanding the enrollment process.

College Support for Foster Youth

Many colleges and universities have programs to support current and former foster youth. For example, in California, The NextUp Program https://nextup.cccco.edu/ and Guardian Scholars.

Kinship care in the foster care system refers to the care of children by relatives.

...Job coaches can help clients and their families locate local kinship programs that support kinship families with resources.

Job Search Strategies

As with other clients, teach youth clients effective job search techniques: Using online job boards, calling employers, networking, asking family and friends for job leads, and utilizing social media platforms.

Interview Preparation

Conduct mock interviews to help youth practice their interview skills. Prepare for the interview by answering common questions confidently, having a thank-you letter ready, and making a positive impression on potential employers.

Mock interviews are discussed in Chapter 6.

Discuss interview attire. If a candidate doesn't have professional clothing or can't afford an interview outfit, many high schools, colleges, churches, or nonprofits offer clothing closets. If no such resource exists in your community, consider starting one at your office.

Mentorship and Networking Opportunities

Connect youth with mentors, role models, and professionals in their fields of interest to provide guidance, support, and networking opportunities. For example, in Southern California, the Orange County Hispanic Youth Chamber of Commerce (OCHYCC) offers valuable resources for young professionals.

https://ochycc.org

Youth Programs

Connect clients with other youth-focused programs that offer additional support and guidance. Some cities and county departments provide civic engagement opportunities, such as Mayor's Youth Advisory Committees or Councils.

...Create a handout of local programs and networks who's aim is to assist youth with resources, employment and job training.

Celebrate Achievements

Celebrate the youth's achievements, milestones, and progress throughout their job search and career development journey to boost confidence and motivation.

Resume and Cover Letter Writing

Assist youth in creating professional resumes and cover letters tailored to their skills and experiences, emphasizing relevant volunteer work, extracurricular activities, and part-time jobs. Explain that a resume is a living document—one that should be updated regularly as they gain new skills and experiences. It should also be customized for each job application.

For high school students with limited work experience, their resumes should highlight their skills, achievements, and involvement in activities that demonstrate their strengths and potential.

Key Elements

Education: Include relevant coursework (if possible)

Extracurricular Activities: Clubs, sports teams, student government, etc. Positions held and key responsibilities or accomplishments

Volunteer Experience: Organization name, location, dates of service, responsibilities and achievements in bullet points.

Skills: Technical skills (e.g., computer software, programming languages), soft skills (e.g., communication, teamwork, problem-solving), languages spoken

Honors and Awards: Academic honors, scholarships, or awards received. Description and date of each award

Certificates: Any relevant certifications (e.g., CPR, First Aid, Microsoft Office Specialist)

Sample Youth Resume

Marie Jaimes

City, State
Phone
Email

Motivated and enthusiastic high school student seeking a part-time position to apply skills in [specific area] while gaining valuable work experience.

Skills

Basic Computer Skills • Bilingual Spanish • Team Player • Customer Service • Self-Motivated Strong Work Ethic • Ability to Work Independently • Attention to Detail

---

Work Experience

2024 - 2024

Cashier, ABC Grocery Store, City, State

- Operated cash register and handled customer transactions efficiently
- Assisted customers with product inquiries and provided excellent service
- Maintained clean and organized checkout area

Volunteer Experience

Volunteer, Local Food Bank, City, State
January 2022 – Present

- Assisted in sorting and packing food donations
- Helped organize community food drives and events

Extracurricular Activities
President, Student Government Association
September 2022 – Present

- Led weekly meetings and organized school events
- Coordinated with faculty and student body to address school issues

---

Education
XYZ High School, City, State

WORKSHOPS AND WEBINARS FOR GROUPS

Consider providing workshops or webinars in group settings (for youth or adults).

Career Planning

Career planning workshops can provide valuable guidance on the career exploration process.

Career planning is discussed in Chapter 13.

Encourage youth to explore various career options by seeking internships, apprenticeship programs, volunteer opportunities, job shadowing, and informational interviews. Additionally, encourage them to attend job fairs and college/career fairs to expand their knowledge and network with potential employers.

...Having recorded webinars available is a great way to save time and energy. Email recording webinars or schedule a live webinar that includes a recorded webinar and provide a live Q&A session.

Other Workshop Topics

- Job Readiness
- Career Planning
- College Planning
- Successful Student Skills
- Volunteerism/Civic Engagement
- Resume Writing
- Preparing for Interviews
- Local Programs
- Financial Literacy
- The Basics of Entrepreneurship

PARTNER WITH PARENTS

Parents play a crucial role in their child's career planning and development. Their influence can shape career choices, aspirations, and attitudes toward work and education. While *family influence* is a common factor in career decisions, its impact varies based on individual circumstances, cultural background, and family dynamics. It is essential for young people to find a balance between respecting their family's influence and pursuing a career that aligns with their own interests and goals.

Job coaches can effectively collaborate with parents of high school-aged clients by fostering open communication, providing guidance, and offering support. A strong partnership between job coaches and parents creates a supportive environment that helps youth become job-ready and succeed in their employment endeavors.

Consent

If the client is under 18, a parent or guardian should sign a consent form allowing the job coach to work with the minor and for the client to receive services from you and your agency.

Family Support

The career planning process can be stressful and overwhelming for young people. Parents and family members play a vital role in providing emotional stability and a safe space for their children to express their fears, anxieties, and hopes about their future careers. They can help their children weigh the pros and cons of different options, consider long-term implications, and make well-rounded decisions that align with their strengths and interests.

Parents also provide essential guidance in exploring career options, setting goals, and making informed decisions. Their life experience and knowledge offer valuable perspectives that help children navigate the complexities of career planning.

Additionally, parental encouragement can boost a child's confidence in pursuing their career interests and ambitions. Positive reinforcement from parents helps children stay motivated and resilient when facing challenges or setbacks in their career journey.

Parental Occupations

Parents serve as role models, and their attitudes toward work, education, and career can significantly influence their child's perspective. When parents demonstrate a strong work ethic and emphasize the value of lifelong learning, children are more likely to adopt similar values.

Many children consider careers that align with their parents' professions, either due to early exposure to those fields or encouragement to follow in their footsteps.

Socioeconomic Factors and Cultural Expectations

Families often influence career choices based on socioeconomic factors, encouraging paths that offer financial stability, security, and upward mobility.

In many cultures, family expectations play a significant role in career decisions, with young people feeling pressured to pursue professions highly valued by their families, such as practicing Medicine.

Involve Parents

Establish regular communication with parents to keep them informed about their child's progress, goals, and the steps being taken to prepare them for employment. This transparency builds trust and ensures alignment among all parties.

Include parents in the goal-setting process by inviting them to participate in discussions about their child's career interests, strengths, and developmental needs. Their insight can help tailor the job coaching plan more effectively.

Encourage parents to actively support their child's job search by assisting with researching job opportunities, practicing interview skills at home, and reinforcing the importance of workplace etiquette and responsibility.

Address Barriers Together

Collaborate with parents to identify and address any barriers to employment their child may face, such as transportation, scheduling conflicts, or balancing work and school commitments. Working together, you can develop solutions that support the youth's job readiness and success.

Educate and Provide Resources

Parents often provide essential resources for career development, such as access to education, extracurricular activities, and networking opportunities. These resources play a crucial role in building the skills and experiences necessary for future success.

Job coaches can also educate parents on the job readiness process, including resume building, interview techniques, and job search strategies. Equipping parents with the right tools and resources empowers them to support their child's path to employment.

Celebrate Successes

Encourage parents to celebrate their child's achievements, such as securing a job interview or employment. This positive reinforcement strengthens their partnership and motivates the youth.

STUDIES ON YOUTH EMPLOYMENT

Work Experience Programs

Research suggests that high school work experience programs help prevent student dropouts by increasing engagement and creating practical connections between education and career goals. Internships, apprenticeships, and other career-focused experiences provide hands-on learning opportunities, allowing students to see the value of their education while preparing for future employment or further studies. Studies show that when students participate in activities that align school with their career aspirations, their motivation and commitment improve—both key factors in dropout prevention.

Source: Institute of Education Sciences. (n.d.). What Works Clearinghouse practice guide. https://ies.ed.gov/ncee/wwc/practiceguide/24

.

Career and Technical Education and Work-Based Learning

According to the National Dropout Prevention Center, career and technical education (CTE) and work-based learning provide alternative pathways for students who may struggle in traditional academic settings, keeping them engaged and preparing them for real-world demands.

Source: National Dropout Prevention Center. Effective Strategies for Dropout Prevention. https://dropoutprevention.org/effective-strategies/

Higher Graduation Rates and Dropout Prevention

High school students with part-time jobs generally have high graduation rates, but the impact of work on academic success depends on the number of hours worked and the nature of their employment. Research shows that students who work fewer than 20 hours per week tend to maintain stable GPAs, with work potentially enhancing time management skills and reinforcing the link between education and income.

Source: Keister, M., & Hall, J. (2010). High school employment and academic achievement: A note for educators. Contemporary Issues in Education Research, 3(1), 109–114.

Potential Partnerships for Job Coaches

- High Schools (Public, private, charter, continuation/alternative education)
- Adult Schools
- Local Community Youth & Recreation Centers
- Nonprofits that serve youth
- Foster Youth Programs
- Juvenile Detention Centers & Probation Offices
- County and City Youth Programs
- Apprenticeship Programs

RESOURCES FOR JOB COACHES

- Apprenticeship USA https://www.apprenticeship.gov/
- Youth Build https://youthbuild.org/
- Virginia Commonwealth University, The Rehabilitation Research and Training Center (RRTC) on Employment of Transition-Age Youth with Disabilities
  https://transition.vcurrtc.org/
- National Technical Assistance Center on Transition
  https://transitionta.org/
- Be Pro Be Proud https://beprobeproud.org/

Associations

- Association for Career & Technical Education
  https://www.acteonline.org/

Personality/Career Aptitude Assessments

- 16 Personalities www.16personalities.com
- My Next Move https://www.mynextmove.org
- ONet Interest Profiler

  https://www.mynextmove.org/explore/ip

- My Skills My Future https://www.myskillsmyfuture.org/

8

Coaching Individuals with Disabilities

- Types of Disabilities
- Ways Disabilities Impact Employment
- Benefits of Employment
- Strategies and Techniques
- Other Supports
- Resources for Job Coaches

Various disabilities can impact employment by affecting job performance, requiring workplace accommodations, and shaping the overall work experience. By understanding and addressing these challenges, job coaches can better support and advocate for their clients.

It is essential to recognize that individuals with disabilities bring unique strengths, abilities, and talents. Creating accessible, inclusive workplaces with appropriate accommodations allows them to thrive and contribute valuable skills and perspectives to diverse teams and organizations.

TYPES OF DISABILITIES

Physical Disabilities

Mobility Impairments: Conditions that impact a person's ability to move, such as spinal cord injuries, multiple sclerosis, muscular dystrophy, and arthritis.

Sensory Impairments. Includes vision impairments (blindness, low vision) and hearing impairments (deafness, hard of hearing).

Cognitive Disabilities

Learning disabilities and conditions that affect information processing, such as dyslexia and dyscalculia.

Intellectual disabilities are conditions like Down syndrome and other developmental disorders that impact intellectual functioning and adaptive behavior.

Psychiatric Disabilities

Mental health disorders are conditions such as depression, anxiety, bipolar disorder, and schizophrenia that can affect concentration, energy levels, and social interactions.

Neurological Disabilities

Epilepsy is a neurological disorder that may affect concentration and physical safety in the workplace.

Traumatic Brain Injury (TBI) is a condition that can impact cognitive function, memory, and physical abilities.

Chronic Illnesses

Conditions like diabetes, cancer, and chronic fatigue syndrome, which can cause fluctuating abilities and may require frequent medical leave or flexible schedules.

Developmental Disabilities

Autism Spectrum Disorder (ASD) is one developmental disability that can impact communication, social interactions, and behavior, often requiring specific accommodations.

Invisible Disabilities

Invisible Disabilities are conditions such as chronic pain, fibromyalgia, and certain autoimmune diseases, which can impact energy levels, mobility, and overall health despite not being immediately visible.

WAYS DISABILITIES IMPACT EMPLOYMENT

Job Performance: Some individuals may require specific adaptations or assistive technologies to perform their job duties effectively.

Workplace Accommodations: Reasonable accommodations, such as modified workstations, flexible schedules, or telecommuting options, may be necessary.

Discrimination and Bias: Individuals with disabilities may face prejudices and discrimination, impacting hiring, promotions, and workplace inclusion.

Accessibility: Physical and digital accessibility barriers may require accessible facilities, technology, and workplace adjustments.

Health and Safety: Specific considerations may be needed to ensure a safe working environment for individuals with certain disabilities.

Training and Support: Additional training for both employees and colleagues can help foster an inclusive and supportive workplace.

BENEFITS OF EMPLOYMENT

Gaining employment offers significant benefits for individuals with disabilities. With the right support, job coaches can help them secure meaningful work and achieve their occupational goals, positively impacting various aspects of their lives.

Financial Independence

Employment provides a steady income, enabling individuals with disabilities to achieve financial self-sufficiency. This stability offers greater independence and reduces reliance on government benefits or family support.

Enhanced Self-Esteem and Confidence

Gainful employment enhances self-worth and confidence, providing a sense of accomplishment and purpose that contributes to overall psychological well-being.

Social Inclusion and Connection

Employment offers opportunities for social interaction and relationship-building with colleagues, helping to reduce feelings of isolation while fostering a sense of belonging and community involvement.

Skill Development and Personal Growth

Jobs provide opportunities to learn new skills, gain experience, and foster both personal and professional growth. Continuous learning and skill development can lead to career advancement and greater job satisfaction.

Improved Mental Health

Engaging in meaningful work can positively impact mental health by reducing symptoms of depression and anxiety. The structure and routine of a job, combined with a sense of purpose, contribute significantly to overall well-being.

Access to Benefits

Many jobs provide benefits such as health insurance, retirement plans, and paid leave. Access to these benefits enhances overall health, ensures financial security, and contributes to a higher quality of life.

Reduced Stigma and Stereotypes

Employment can challenge societal perceptions about the abilities of individuals with disabilities. Visible success stories in the workforce help reduce stigma and promote a more inclusive society.

Increased Independence and Autonomy

Employment empowers individuals with disabilities to make independent choices and lead self-sufficient lives. This autonomy strengthens their ability to manage daily affairs and shape their own future.

Contribution to the Economy

Employed individuals contribute to the economy through taxes and spending, supporting community development and sustaining public services.

Role Modeling and Inspiration

Employed individuals with disabilities can serve as role models, inspiring and motivating others in similar situations to pursue their career goals and believe in their potential.

Legal and Social Rights

Gaining employment often involves awareness and advocacy for workplace accommodations and anti-discrimination rights. This advocacy can drive broader societal changes, enhancing accessibility and inclusivity across various sectors.

STRATEGIES AND TECHNIQUES

By employing effective strategies and techniques, job coaches can support individuals in securing and maintaining meaningful employment, ultimately enhancing their independence and quality of life.

Workplace Accommodations

Enacted in 1990, the Americans with Disabilities Act (ADA) is a landmark civil rights law that prohibits discrimination against individuals with disabilities in all areas of public life, including employment, education, transportation, and access to public and private spaces. Its purpose is to ensure equal rights and opportunities for people with disabilities. The ADA mandates reasonable workplace accommodations, accessibility standards for public spaces, and effective communication for individuals with hearing, vision, or speech disabilities, fostering inclusion and equal participation in society.

Job coaches working with individuals with disabilities should have a strong understanding of the ADA and be able to educate clients about their rights and available accommodations. Necessary accommodations may include adaptive equipment, modified workstations, flexible scheduling, or telecommuting options. These efforts are essential for enabling clients to perform their jobs effectively and comfortably while reducing barriers to employment.

Individualized Assessment

Conduct thorough assessments to understand the client's abilities, interests, and specific needs. Utilize tools such as interest inventories and vocational evaluations. The agency you work for may also provide specific vocational assessments and processes at the start of services.

Collaborative Goal Setting

Work with clients to set realistic, achievable goals using frameworks like SMART. Provide clear direction and motivation, ensuring that goals are meaningful and attainable. Encourage clients to identify their 'why'—understanding their personal motivation can help them persevere through challenges and stay committed to their goals.

Goal setting is discussed in Chapter 2.

Skill Development

Equip clients with the necessary competencies to excel in their chosen roles by assessing their need for training. This may include formal programs or short-term skill development, such as soft skills (e.g., communication, teamwork) or hard skills (e.g., technical abilities, computer literacy).

Job Matching and Customization

We can enhance job satisfaction and success by ensuring a strong fit between clients and their roles. Strive to match clients with jobs that align with their skills, strengths, interests, and career aspirations.

Job Search Assistance

Teach effective job search strategies, including resume writing, job applications, and interview preparation. Provide guidance on navigating online job boards and leveraging networking opportunities.

Building Employer Partnerships

Broaden job opportunities and foster inclusive hiring practices by building strong relationships with employers to create meaningful opportunities for clients. Educate employers on the benefits of hiring individuals with disabilities and inform them about available support resources to facilitate a successful work environment.

Utilizing Assistive Technology

Improve accessibility and efficiency by introducing clients to assistive technologies that enhance job performance, such as screen readers, voice recognition software, or ergonomic tools. Provide training to help clients effectively use these tools, enabling them to overcome challenges and perform tasks with greater ease.

Advocacy and Empowerment

Foster independence and self-confidence, enabling clients to navigate their careers with autonomy. Empower them to advocate for their rights and workplace needs by providing education on disability rights and self-advocacy.

Peer Support and Mentoring

Support clients by connecting them with peer support groups or mentors who have successfully navigated similar challenges. Foster a sense of community and belonging by providing encouragement and sharing experiences.

Ongoing Support and Follow-Up

Promote long-term success and job retention by offering consistent support through regular check-ins, mentorship, and problem-solving assistance. Continuously monitor progress and proactively address any challenges that arise.

OTHER SUPPORTS

IEPs and 504 Plans

An Individualized Education Program (IEP) is a legal document designed to ensure that students with disabilities in the United States receive specialized instruction and services tailored to their unique educational needs. Students who qualify for special education services under the Individuals with Disabilities Education Act (IDEA) are required to have an IEP.

Developed through a collaborative process involving educators, parents, and other professionals—such as counselors or specialists—the IEP outlines the student's specific learning goals, the services and accommodations that will be provided, and the strategies for monitoring and measuring progress. The document is reviewed at least annually and must be updated to reflect the student's evolving needs.

A 504 Plan, based on Section 504 of the Rehabilitation Act of 1973, ensures that students with disabilities receive equal access to educational opportunities. It provides necessary supports, such as extended time on tests, modified classroom seating, or assistive technology, allowing students to fully participate in school activities. While a 504 Plan helps students succeed academically by removing barriers, it differs from an IEP, which focuses on specialized instruction and services.

If your client has an IEP, you may be asked to collaborate with educators to help support their educational goals.

Source: Schultz, S. (2022, December). *Differences between a 504 Plan and an Individualized Education Program (IEP)*. Retrieved from https://www.understood.org/articles/en/differences-between-a-504-plan-and-an-individualized-education-program-iep

Assistance for College Students

If your client is attending a college or university, ask whether they are registered with the school's Center for Students with Disabilities.

These types of centers may be able to assist with:

- Requesting accommodations for classes
- Assistive Technology, such as requesting alternate formats, such as Braille or electronic text, of textbooks or course materials
- Arranging for in-class note-takers
- Other resources

Other Agencies

Each state has a Vocational Rehabilitation (VR) Department, which provides vocational rehabilitation and other services to individuals with disabilities, helping them gain employment in a competitive labor market and live independently.

States also have Departments of Developmental Services, which ensure that individuals with developmental disabilities have opportunities to make choices and live independently. Additionally, some states have Regional Centers that offer case management services for people with developmental disabilities.

There may also be nonprofits and for-profit organizations in your community that support individuals with disabilities by providing work experiences and life skills training.

RESOURCES FOR JOB COACHES

- Rehabilitation Services Administration – State Vocational Rehabilitation Agencies https://rsa.ed.gov/about/states
- U.S. Department of Justice, Civil Rights Division ADA.gov https://www.ada.gov/
- Administration for Community Living https://acl.gov/programs/centers-independent-living/list-cils-and-spils
- The National Association of State Directors of Developmental Disabilities Services https://www.nasddds.org/state-agencies/
- Ability Magazine https://abilitymagazine.com/
- The Job Accommodation Network (JAN) www.askjan.org
- Supplemental Security Income (SSI) Work Incentives https://ssa.gov/ssi/text-work-ussi.htm
- Social Security Administration – Ticket 2 Work Program https://www.ssa.gov/work/
- Vocational Rehabilitation Technical Assistance Center for Quality Employment https://tacqe.com/
- National Institute of Child Health and Human Development. (n.d.). Types of assistive technology. Retrieved from https://www.nichd.nih.gov/health/topics/rehabtech/conditioninfo/device

9

Coaching Veterans

- Veteran Affairs
- Barriers to Employment
- Providing Support
- Resources for Job Coaches

A *Veteran* is an individual who has served in their country's armed forces, including branches such as the Army, Navy, Air Force, Marines, or Coast Guard. Veterans may have served during wartime or peacetime and may be retired, discharged, or have completed their term of service.

Through their military experience, veterans often acquire specialized skills and training. Their service and sacrifices are widely recognized and honored by society, with various support services available to assist them in their post-military lives.

VETERAN AFFAIRS

The Department of Veterans Affairs (VA) is a U.S. government agency dedicated to providing comprehensive support and services to military veterans. The VA offers a wide range of resources, including healthcare through VA hospitals and clinics, mental health support, disability compensation, and rehabilitation services.

Additionally, the VA provides education benefits, such as the Government Issue Bill (GI Bill), which helps veterans and their families afford higher education and training programs. The agency also assists with home loans, vocational training, employment services, and pension programs.

Through these extensive offerings, the VA strives to ensure that veterans receive the care and resources they need to successfully transition to civilian life and maintain their well-being.

Vocational Rehabilitation

Through the VA, Vocational Rehabilitation Counselors (VRCs) provide comprehensive support to veterans with service-connected disabilities, helping them transition from military to civilian employment.

These counselors conduct individualized assessments to identify veterans' skills, interests, and any barriers to employment. They assist in translating military experience into marketable skills, crafting effective resumes, and preparing for job interviews. Additionally, they connect veterans with education and training opportunities, leveraging benefits like the GI Bill to enhance their qualifications.

VRCs also provide guidance on accessing VA resources, including vocational rehabilitation and employment programs, healthcare services, and support for physical and mental health needs. Through personalized career counseling and ongoing support, they empower veterans to achieve their career goals and secure sustainable, meaningful employment.

BARRIERS TO EMPLOYMENT

Veterans often face unique challenges when transitioning to civilian life, including securing employment, accessing healthcare, and managing the physical and mental health impacts of their service. Overcoming these barriers requires a comprehensive approach that includes tailored support, specialized training programs, mental health services, and initiatives to educate employers on the value of hiring veterans.

Translating Military Skills to Civilian Jobs

Veterans may struggle to articulate how their military experience and skills translate to civilian job roles. This can result in employers undervaluing their qualifications, making it more difficult to secure suitable positions.

Mental Health Challenges

Mental health conditions such as Post-Traumatic Stress Disorder (PTSD), anxiety, and depression can impact veterans' job performance and workplace interactions. These challenges may lead to absenteeism, difficulty concentrating, and strained workplace relationships, affecting their ability to thrive in a civilian work environment.

Sources: U.S. Department of Health and Human Services, National Institutes of Health. (2023). Post-traumatic stress disorder (PTSD) (NIH Publication No. 23-MH-8124). Retrieved from https://www.nimh.nih.gov/health/publications/post-traumatic-stress-disorder-ptsd

Physical Disabilities

Injuries sustained during service can result in physical disabilities, which may limit the types of jobs veterans can perform. As a result, they may require workplace accommodations or encounter discrimination due to their physical limitations.

Lack of Civilian Work Experience

Some veterans may have limited or no civilian work experience, making it difficult to compete with candidates who have more directly relevant backgrounds. This lack of experience can also create challenges in adapting to civilian workplace norms and securing employment.

Cultural Adjustment

Transitioning from the structured military environment to a more varied and less regimented civilian workplace can be challenging. Veterans may struggle to adapt to different work cultures, expectations, and communication styles as they adjust to civilian employment.

Gaps in Employment

Time spent in military service or managing medical issues can lead to employment gaps, which employers may perceive negatively. These gaps may raise concerns about a veteran's job stability or continuous workforce engagement, making it more challenging to secure employment.

Credential Recognition

Military certifications and training may not always be recognized or valued by civilian employers. As a result, veterans may need to obtain additional certifications or training to meet civilian job requirements, despite having extensive experience.

Discrimination and Stigma

Misconceptions and biases about veterans, particularly those with mental health conditions, can lead to discrimination in hiring and workplace practices. This may limit job opportunities and contribute to a hostile or unwelcoming work environment.

Limited Networking Opportunities

Veterans may have limited professional networks in the civilian job market, which can hinder their job search and career advancement. Since networking plays a crucial role in securing employment, the lack of connections may create additional challenges in finding job opportunities.

Financial Pressures

Financial instability or debt accumulated during or after military service can add significant stress. This pressure may force veterans to accept jobs that do not align with their skills or career goals, simply to make ends meet.

Geographic Relocation

Frequent relocations during military service may lead veterans to settle in areas with limited job opportunities. These geographic constraints can restrict access to employment options and hinder career advancement.

PROVIDING SUPPORT

Job coaches play a crucial role in assisting veterans by addressing their unique needs and leveraging their strengths. By implementing targeted strategies, job coaches can provide comprehensive support, helping veterans navigate the transition from military to civilian employment and achieve long-term career success.

Understanding Veterans' Backgrounds

Develop a comprehensive understanding of a veteran's military experience, including their skills, training, and any challenges faced during and after service. This insight helps translate military skills into civilian job requirements and identify relevant career paths.

Translating Military Experience

Help veterans articulate their military skills, experiences, and qualifications in a way that civilian employers understand. Enhance their resumes and job applications to showcase their capabilities in a manner that resonates with potential employers.

Career Counseling and Goal Setting

Assist veterans in identifying their career interests and setting realistic, achievable goals. Provide direction and motivation, ensuring career paths align with their skills and aspirations.

Encourage veterans to define their "why" - understanding the deeper motivation behind their goals. This clarity helps them persevere through challenges and stay committed to their career journey.

Goal setting is discussed in Chapter 2.

Skill Development and Training

Identify skills gaps and recommend training programs to bridge them. Equip veterans with the necessary competencies to succeed in the civilian workforce.

Job Search Assistance

Guide veterans on effective job search strategies, including networking, utilizing job boards, and approaching potential employers. These strategies improve job search effectiveness and increase the likelihood of securing suitable employment.

Resume and Cover Letter Writing

Help veterans craft resumes and cover letters that highlight their strengths and experiences in a way that appeals to civilian employers. Ensure their application materials are compelling and accurately reflect their qualifications.

Interview Preparation

Conduct mock interviews and provide constructive feedback to boost veterans' confidence and interview performance.

Interviewing is discussed in Chapter 6.

Connecting with Employers

Develop relationships with employers who are committed to hiring veterans and understand the value they bring. This fosters inclusive hiring practices and creates more job opportunities for veterans.

Provide Resources

Guide veterans in accessing community and veteran-specific resources, including the GI Bill, vocational rehabilitation programs, and veteran employment services. Help them leverage these resources to support their career development and smooth transition into civilian employment.

Providing Ongoing Support

Offer continuous support through regular check-ins, mentorship, and problem-solving assistance. Ensure long-term success and job retention by addressing any issues that arise and providing necessary guidance.

Addressing Physical and Mental Health Needs

Be aware of any physical or mental health issues that might impact their employment. Encourage veterans to seek appropriate healthcare providers and support services. Ensure that their health needs are managed effectively, supporting their overall well-being and job performance.

Creating a Supportive Network

Facilitate connections with veteran support groups, peer mentors, and other veterans in the workforce. Provide a sense of community and shared experience, which can be especially important for veterans adjusting to civilian life.

Potential Partnerships for Job Coaches

- Veteran Affairs VR Counselors & Career Centers
- Nonprofits that serve Veterans

RESOURCES FOR JOB COACHES

- Veteran Affairs – Careers and Employment
  https://www.va.gov/careers-employment/

- National Veterans' Training Institute
  https://www.nvti.org/

- U.S. Department of Veterans Affairs, Veteran Readiness and Employment (Chapter 31)
  https://www.va.gov/careers-employment/vocational-rehabilitation/

- U.S. Small Business Administration, Veterans Business Outreach Center (VBOC) program
  https://www.sba.gov/local-assistance/resource-partners/veterans-business-outreach-center-vboc-program

- Trauma Informed Care, Implementations Resource Center
  https://www.traumainformedcare.chcs.org/

10

Coaching Justice-Involved

- Common Barriers and Challenges
- Strategies and Techniques
- Resources for Job Coaches

Justice-Involved or *Justice-Impacted* individuals are those who have interacted with the criminal justice system, whether through arrest, conviction, incarceration, probation, or parole. This term includes individuals currently serving sentences, those recently released, and those under community supervision.

The *Re-Entry* population refers specifically to individuals transitioning from incarceration back into society.

Justice-involved individuals often face significant barriers to reintegration, including difficulties in securing employment, housing, education, and social services. These challenges can impact their ability to successfully rebuild their lives after their involvement with the justice system.

Supporting justice-impacted individuals requires a nuanced approach that addresses their unique challenges, experiences, and employment barriers. Effective job coaching can help them develop the skills, confidence, and opportunities needed for successful workforce reintegration.

COMMON BARRIERS AND CHALLENGES

When job coaching individuals with a criminal history, it's essential to approach the process with sensitivity, understanding, and a strategic mindset to help them overcome employment barriers.

By keeping these considerations in mind, job coaches can provide effective and compassionate support, helping individuals secure meaningful employment while fostering their long-term success and well-being.

Stigma

Stigma is a negative social attitude or belief that leads to discrimination, prejudice, or exclusion based on specific characteristics or circumstances, such as mental illness, a criminal history, or substance use. It often results in unfair judgment, devaluation, and marginalization, creating barriers to opportunities and preventing individuals from seeking help or reintegrating into society.

Individuals with criminal histories frequently encounter significant stigma from employers, coworkers, and society. As a coach, approach your work with empathy and a nonjudgmental attitude to build trust and encourage openness.

Help your clients develop strategies to address stigma proactively. Guide them in crafting a positive narrative that highlights their growth, resilience, and strengths. Encourage them to reframe their experiences, emphasizing lessons learned, personal development, and a commitment to positive change.

Criminal Records

People can have various types of criminal records, ranging from minor offenses to serious crimes. These records typically include misdemeanors, which are less severe offenses such as petty theft, vandalism, or disorderly conduct, often resulting in fines, community service, or short jail terms. More serious offenses are classified as felonies, which include crimes like burglary, assault, drug trafficking, and violent crimes such as robbery, rape, or murder. Felony convictions generally lead to longer prison sentences and more severe legal consequences.

Additionally, some individuals may have records related to drug offenses, driving under the influence (DUI), or other traffic-related violations. Juvenile records, which pertain to crimes committed as minors, are often handled differently—some may be sealed or expunged upon reaching adulthood.

The type of criminal record a person has can significantly impact their access to employment, housing, and other opportunities. As a coach, stay informed about the legal implications of criminal records in employment, including background checks, "Ban the Box" laws, and rights related to expungement or record sealing.

Provide clients with accurate information and resources to help them navigate these legal challenges. Guide them on how to address their criminal record with potential employers honestly and strategically, focusing on accountability, personal growth, and their readiness to contribute positively to the workplace.

...Refer clients to local legal aid offices. Some charges can be dropped to a lesser charge, expunged or sealed.

Limited Access to Education and Employment

Conduct a comprehensive assessment of your client's skills, experiences, and potential. Identify any gaps in education or job skills and explore opportunities for training, certification, or further education to enhance their employability.

Help them target employers known for being open to hiring individuals with criminal histories. Develop job search strategies that focus on industries or roles where their skills are in demand and where their background may be less of a barrier.

Encourage them to build a strong support network, including mentors, advocates, and professionals who can offer guidance, referrals, and positive references. A supportive network can play a crucial role in rebuilding confidence and opening doors to new opportunities.

Potential Trauma

Recognize that many individuals with criminal histories may have experienced trauma or PTSD. Be sensitive to signs of trauma and approach coaching in a way that avoids re-traumatization. Seek opportunities to expand your knowledge of Trauma-Informed Care to provide more effective support.

Encourage clients to access mental health resources, such as counseling or therapy, to help them manage trauma-related symptoms. Ensure they have the necessary support to maintain emotional stability throughout the job search and employment process.

Work with them to develop coping strategies for managing stress, anxiety, and potential triggers that may arise during their job search or in the workplace. Equipping them with these tools can improve their confidence, resilience, and long-term success.

Source: Center for Health Care Strategies. (n.d.). What is trauma-informed care? Retrieved from https://www.traumainformedcare.chcs.org/what-is-trauma-informed-care/

What Employers Can Acquire

- Credit Reports
- Criminal / Arrest Records
- Worker Compensation Records
- References
- Medical History
- Education Records
- Check writing History
- Tenant History
- DMV Driving/Vehicle Registration Records
- Insurance Claims Reports
- Immigration Records
- Military Records
- Social Media

STRATEGIES AND TECHNIQUES

Building Trust and Rapport

Establish a trusting and supportive relationship with clients by acknowledging their past experiences and demonstrating non-judgmental support. Building trust is essential for fostering openness and engagement in the coaching process.

Cultural Sensitivity and Empathy

Approach coaching with empathy and cultural sensitivity, recognizing the diverse backgrounds, experiences, and needs of justice-involved individuals. A tailored, understanding approach helps create a safe and supportive environment.

Legal Barriers and Rights

Provide clients with accurate information and support regarding legal barriers to employment. Help them understand the impact of criminal records, explore expungement options, and navigate their rights under fair hiring laws.

Stay informed about local laws and regulations regarding the disclosure of criminal history during the hiring process. In some jurisdictions, employers may be restricted from asking about certain types of convictions or arrests. Ensuring clients are aware of their rights can empower them to advocate for themselves effectively.

Discussing Gaps in Employment

Employment gaps are discussed in Chapter 6.

Disclosure of Criminal History

Help clients make informed decisions about disclosing their criminal history to employers while navigating the reintegration process into the workforce.

Encourage clients to practice disclosure strategies with a friend, family member, mentor, or job coach through mock interviews and by proofreading cover letters or personal narratives.

Guide them in writing a clear, honest narrative and practicing responses to common interview questions. Anticipating employer concerns and preparing thoughtful answers can demonstrate their commitment to openness and transparency.

Advise clients to wait until they have built rapport with the interviewer and the employer has shown interest in hiring them. Disclosing too early may create unnecessary barriers.

Help them identify an appropriate moment to bring up their criminal history—ideally later in the conversation, after they have highlighted their skills, qualifications, and value to the company.

Honesty and Integrity

Emphasize the importance of truthfulness when completing paperwork and discussing their background. Misrepresenting or concealing a criminal history can have serious consequences, including potential termination if discovered later. Always be truthful about your criminal history while framing the conversation in a way that highlights personal growth and positive change.

Key Strategies for Discussing Your Criminal History

- Provide context by helping the employer understand the circumstances surrounding the incident.

- Take responsibility by expressing remorse and acknowledging accountability for past actions.

- Highlight personal growth, by sharing what you've learned from the experience and how it has contributed to your development.

- Show proactive change by discussing steps you've taken to address the issue, such as completing rehabilitation programs, obtaining certifications, or engaging in community service.

- Emphasize progress by showcasing your commitment to self-improvement and maintaining a law-abiding, positive lifestyle.

- Focus on the present and future by shifting the conversation toward your current skills, strengths, and contributions you can bring to the company.

- Tailor your approach, every situation is unique. Adapt your discussion based on the job, the employer, and the nature of your past offense.

- Demonstrate humility and openness by approaching the conversation with confidence, honesty, and a focus on how you can add value to the organization.

Examples:

"Eight years ago, I was convicted of possessing a controlled substance. I served my time and am now on parole. I took part in an addiction program and am now drug-free. Since my conviction, I have earned my GED and cosmetology license. I have reconnected with my family and am living with my parents. They are incredibly loving and supportive. My conviction was a mistake I made, but I have turned my life around. It won't happen again."

"I served .... years of time at a correctional facility ....years ago.

Here's what I learned from it .... (2-3 lessons)

Here's how I changed my life ... (2-3 examples)

Here's how I'll bring value to your company ... (2-3 ways you'll contribute)"

Assessing Skills and Strengths

Assist clients in identifying their transferable skills, strengths, and experiences that align with employment opportunities, regardless of their justice involvement.

Job Readiness Preparation

Provide your clients with support in developing essential job readiness skills, including resume writing, interview preparation, effective communication, and workplace etiquette.

...Encourage clients to obtain positive personal and professional references and letters of recommendation that highlight their skills, accomplishments, character, etc. After an interview, applicants can offer letters of recommendation or reference letters from people who can vouch for their character and work ethic.

When applying for jobs, applicants should familiarize themselves with the company's hiring policies regarding criminal backgrounds checks. Some employers have specific guidelines or restrictions, so it's important to research this information before interviewing.

When reviewing job advertisements, check if the requirements mention background checks or a specific hiring criterion. Understanding these details can help you prepare for the conversation.

Access to Employment Opportunities

Provide resources and support to access employment opportunities, including job search assistance, vocational training programs, and job placement services.

Some community job centers have representatives who specifically work with formerly incarcerated individuals. Locate job centers: www.careeronestop.org

This online job board, www.honestjobs.com – are for individuals with a criminal record.

Know which local employers are felony-friendly.

Many employers conduct background checks. Job postings or company human resource websites often specify eligibility requirements. It's essential for job coaches and individuals with criminal histories to understand which industries or roles may have restrictions.

Certain fields, such as banks, schools, law enforcement, and government agencies, often have strict hiring policies regarding applicants with criminal records. Additionally, some medical professions requiring state-issued licenses may impose restrictions on individuals with felony convictions.

Researching these requirements in advance can help job seekers focus on realistic employment opportunities while exploring options for record expungement or alternative career paths.

Building Self-Esteem and Confidence

Help clients develop self-esteem and confidence by recognizing their strengths, accomplishments, and potential contributions to the workforce. Encouraging a positive mindset can empower them to pursue opportunities with determination and resilience.

Supporting Continued Education and Skill Development

Encourage higher education and skill development to enhance their employability and career advancement prospects.

If a client is attending college, guide them toward campus programs, career services, or support groups that can provide mentorship, networking opportunities, and additional resources to support their success.

Addressing Substance Use and Mental Health Needs

Recognize the intersection of justice involvement with substance use disorders (SUD) and mental health issues. Provide referrals and support for accessing treatment and support services.

SUD is discussed in Chapter 11.

Building a Support Network

Connect clients with supportive networks, peer mentors, and community resources that can provide additional support and guidance.

...Find local programs and networks that aim at supporting Justice Impacted and the Re-Entry population with resources, employment, and job training.

Advocacy and Systemic Change

Various advocacy efforts promote policy changes and systemic reforms to remove structural barriers to employment for justice-impacted individuals. Initiatives such as "Ban the Box" and fair chance hiring policies aim to create more equitable hiring practices.

Continued Support and Follow-Up

As with all clients, provide ongoing support and follow-up to help them overcome challenges, celebrate achievements, and sustain long-term success in the workforce.

Employer Benefits

The Work Opportunity Tax Credit (WOTC) provides tax incentives to employers who hire low-income ex-offenders, encouraging fair hiring practices.

The Federal Bonding Program offers insurance to employers concerned about theft or dishonesty, providing financial protection and peace of mind when hiring justice-impacted individuals.

Employers can call 1-877-US2-JOBS for more information on these programs and how to participate.

Potential Partnerships for Job Coaches

- Parole & Probation Offices (for adult and juvenile)
- Workforce Representatives who assist re-entry population
- Nonprofits that serve justice-involved
- Legal Aid offices

RESOURCES FOR JOB COACHES

- Career One Stop

https://www.careeronestop.org/ExOffender/Site/site-map.aspx

- National Institute of Corrections—Transition and Workforce Development

https://nicic.gov/projects/transition-and-offender-workforce-development

- Fair Chance Licensing Project

https://csgjusticecenter.org/projects/fair-chance-licensing/state-by-state-licensing-maps/

- National Inventory of Collateral Consequences of Conviction

https://niccc.nationalreentryresourcecenter.org/

- Restoration of Rights Project

https://ccresourcecenter.org/state-restoration-profiles/50-state-comparisoncomparison-of-criminal-records-in-licensing-and-employment/

- Department of Labor
  https://www.dol.gov/agencies/eta/reentry/grantees

- National H.I.R.E Network https://clearinghouse.lac.org/

- Work Opportunity Tax Credit
  https://www.dol.gov/agencies/eta/wotc

- The Federal Bonding Program https://bonds4jobs.com/

- Lawhelp.org https://www.lawhelp.org/

Job Search Engines

- Honest Jobs www.honestjobs.com

Associations

- The National Association of Reentry Professionals
  www.thenarp.org

11

Coaching Individuals in Recovery

- The Recovery Journey
- Addressing Barriers
- Strategies and Techniques
- Resources for Job Coaches

THE RECOVERY JOURNEY

Recovery from substance use is a journey that encompasses physical, emotional, and psychological healing. The stages of recovery vary—one individual may have been sober for 10 years, while another may have just completed a 30 to 90-day residential inpatient treatment program. As job coaches, it is essential to respect each person's progress and the challenges they may face in their recovery journey.

If you work in a community job center, assist individuals in re-entry programs, or are employed at a drug treatment facility, you may have the opportunity to support people in recovery.

In some cases, you may have no formal training in working with individuals in recovery yet find yourself coaching someone referred by a treatment center or a client who discloses that they are in recovery and attend Alcoholics Anonymous (AA) or Narcotics Anonymous (NA) meetings. Job coaching for individuals in recovery requires a supportive and understanding approach—one that acknowledges their unique challenges, strengths, and goals.

Co-occurring Conditions

It's important to recognize that individuals in recovery often experience co-occurring disabilities, which may include mental health disorders such as depression, anxiety, or PTSD, as well as physical disabilities resulting from prolonged substance use or unrelated health conditions. These co-occurring disabilities can complicate the recovery process, requiring integrated and comprehensive treatment approaches that address both addiction and the additional challenges.

ADDRESSING BARRIERS

During the initial assessment, you will likely identify barriers to employment, such as stigma, limited job skills, gaps in employment history, and legal issues.

Stigma

Using recovery-oriented language and addressing stigma is essential. Job coaches can educate clients about their rights as individuals in recovery or as persons with disabilities. They can also guide clients on how to disclose their disabilities in a way that focuses on strengths, skills, growth, and accomplishments rather than negative experiences or personal challenges. This approach can help build self-esteem and resilience.

Limited Job Skills

Assess the skills, degrees, or certifications that would help your client qualify for their desired job. Do they need a high school diploma, certification, degree, work experience, or computer skills? Identifying these requirements can help clients develop a clear path toward employment.

Gaps in Employment

Help your client address employment gaps when speaking with employers. If asked about these gaps in an interview, they can respond with something like, "I was dealing with a health issue that has since been resolved."

Employment gaps is discussed in Chapter 6.

Legal Issues

Discuss which jobs require background checks and which positions have disqualifying factors for individuals with misdemeanors or felonies. Provide clients with legal aid resources, as some records may be eligible for expungement or sealing, and certain charges may be eligible for reduction.

Disclosing criminal history is discussed in Chapter 10.

Jobs Can Trigger Relapse

Certain jobs pose a higher risk of triggering relapse for individuals in recovery due to the work environment and associated stressors. High-risk industries include:

- Hospitality
- Healthcare
- Construction & Manual Labor
- Transportation
- Corporate & High-Stress Jobs
- Retail & Service Jobs
- Creative & Freelance Work
- Entertainment Industry
- Social Event-Driven Roles

Given these risks, individuals in recovery should be mindful of workplace environments, seek supportive employers, establish coping strategies, and communicate their needs to job coaches and supervisors. Proactive planning can help mitigate risks and support long-term sobriety.

Questions to Ask Clients

Recovery Status

- *How far along are you in your recovery journey?*
- *What support systems do you currently have in place for your recovery?*

Impact of Work on Recovery

- *How do you feel about balancing work with your recovery process?*
- *Are there any particular job environments that you think could support or hinder your recovery?*

Triggers and Stressors

- *Are there specific work-related situations or tasks that could be triggering for you?*
- *How do you typically manage stress, and what support might you need in a work environment to handle stress effectively?*

Support Needs

- *What kind of ongoing support do you think would be helpful for you in maintaining both your job and your recovery?*

- *Are there specific resources or accommodations that have been beneficial for you in the past?*

Relapse Prevention

- *Do you have a relapse prevention plan, and how can your job support this plan?*
- *What signs or situations should we be aware of that might indicate you're struggling in your recovery?*

Work-Life Balance

- *How important is work-life balance to you in supporting your recovery?*
- *What activities outside of work help you stay focused and positive in your recovery?*

STRATEGIES AND TECHNIQUES

Get Well Jobs

A *Get-Well Job* refers to employment that supports an individual's recovery from a mental health condition or substance use disorder. These jobs provide structure, purpose, and a sense of accomplishment, recognizing that meaningful work contributes to a person's identity, self-worth, and social connection—key factors in the recovery process.

The nature of a get-well job varies based on an individual's interests, abilities, and treatment goals. It may involve part-time or full-time employment, volunteer work, or participation in vocational training programs. The primary goal is to intentionally select a job that promotes overall health, stability, and personal growth.

In many cases, a get-well job serves as a stepping stone to more competitive or long-term employment opportunities. It offers a supportive environment where individuals can build skills, regain confidence, and gradually reintegrate into the workforce as they progress in their recovery journey.

Collaboration with Recovery Services

Your workplace may already have partnerships with agencies that offer recovery services, or you may need to identify local resources to share with your clients.

12-Step Programs

12-step programs are support groups designed to help individuals overcome addictions, compulsions, and other behavioral challenges. The most well-known of these is Alcoholics Anonymous (AA), founded in 1935. The 12-step model has since been adapted for various other addictions and issues, including Narcotics Anonymous (NA), Gamblers Anonymous (GA), and Overeaters Anonymous (OA).

The 12 steps serve as guiding principles for recovery, emphasizing personal growth and self-awareness. They involve admitting powerlessness over addiction, recognizing a higher power, conducting a moral inventory, acknowledging past wrongs, making amends, and offering support to others facing similar struggles. These programs promote spiritual awakening and personal transformation.

Meetings provide a supportive environment where members share experiences, offer mutual encouragement, and foster a sense of accountability. The emphasis on anonymity ensures a safe and confidential space for individuals to seek help without fear of judgment.

Positive Impact of Faith and Spirituality

Research suggests that spirituality and religious involvement can serve as protective factors in addiction recovery. Studies indicate that individuals who engage in spiritual or religious practices often report higher motivation to maintain sobriety, greater resilience to stress, and improved emotional well-being.

A 2016 review published in the Journal of Religion and Health found that faith-based interventions were associated with reduced substance use, improved coping strategies, and enhanced social support for individuals in recovery.

SOURCE: Grim, B.J., Grim, M.E. Belief, Behavior, and Belonging: How Faith is Indispensable in Preventing and Recovering from Substance Abuse. *J Relig Health* 58, 1713–1750 (2019). https://doi.org/10.1007/s10943-019-00876-w

Additionally, some studies suggest that individuals participating in 12-step programs with a spiritual or religious foundation tend to have higher abstinence rates. Faith-based programs may be especially beneficial for those with a strong religious background or individuals seeking spiritual growth as part of their recovery journey.

SOURCE: Burnett, Rhonda G. (2014). *Faith-Based Programs in the Treatment of Substance Abuse*. Research Papers, Graduate School, Southern Illinois University Carbondale. Available in OpenSIUC.

Building Trust and Rapport

Establishing a trusting, non-judgmental relationship with clients is essential. Acknowledging their past experiences while demonstrating empathy and support fosters a positive and productive coaching environment.

Assessing Skills and Interests

Help individuals in recovery identify their skills, strengths, and interests to explore career options that align with their recovery goals and long-term aspirations.

Job Readiness Preparation

Provide clients with essential job readiness skills, including resume writing, interview preparation, effective communication, and workplace etiquette. Equipping them with these tools increases their confidence and employability.

Managing Disclosure

Assist clients in making informed decisions about disclosing their recovery status to employers. If they choose to disclose, guide them on how to communicate their experiences in a way that highlights their readiness for employment and commitment to recovery.

When addressing employment gaps due to substance use or treatment, clients can say, *"I was dealing with a health situation that has since been resolved."*

Access to Supportive Employment

Connect clients with employers and industries that provide supportive work environments, such as those offering peer support programs, flexible scheduling, and accommodations for recovery-related needs.

...Create a handout with a list of programs in your community that assist people in recovery. Various programs may be connected to county departments.

Addressing Relapse Prevention

Your role may require incorporating relapse prevention strategies into job coaching sessions. This includes helping clients identify triggers, develop coping skills, and access support services to maintain their recovery while employed. You may also ask clients if they have a Relapse Prevention Plan in place. However, some employers may require a focus solely on job readiness activities—if unsure, consult with your employer for guidance.

Encouraging a Support Network

A strong support network is essential for individuals in recovery. Encourage clients to build connections with peers, mentors, sponsors, and recovery resources that can provide ongoing guidance and support throughout their employment journey.

Promoting Self-Care and Well-Being

Emphasize the importance of self-care practices, stress management techniques, and healthy lifestyle choices. These factors play a critical role in maintaining overall well-being, resilience, and long-term employment success.

Providing Continued Support and Follow-Up

As with all clients, offer ongoing encouragement, support, and follow-up to help address challenges or setbacks. Celebrating successes and milestones along the way can reinforce progress and boost confidence.

Potential Partnerships for Job Coaches

- Treatment Centers
- Agencies that host group meetings
- Behavioral Health Departments
- Community Health Workers/Promotores
- Peer Support Specialists
- Faith-Based Programs

RESOURCES FOR JOB COACHES

- The Substance Abuse and Mental Health Services Administration www.samhsa.gov
- Find Treatment https://findtreatment.gov/locator
- Alcoholics Anonymous https://www.aa.org
- Narcotics Anonymous https://www.na.org
- Support for family and friends https://al-anon.org
- Celebrate Recovery https://celebraterecovery.com

12

Job Retention

- Strategies and Techniques
- Long-term Career Success
- Common Employer Expectations
- Workplace Conflict
- Resources for Job Coaches

Job coaches play a vital role in not only helping clients retain employment but also in supporting their growth and career advancement. By offering personalized guidance tailored to each individual's unique needs, job coaches empower clients to thrive in the workplace and achieve long-term success.

STRATEGIES AND TECHNIQUES

Job coaches help new employees understand their job responsibilities, workplace culture, and expectations. They assist clients in navigating workplace dynamics, fostering relationships with colleagues, and adjusting to their new environment.

To keep clients motivated and engaged, job coaches emphasize the value and impact of their new roles. They provide support during personal or professional challenges that could affect job retention.

Schedule regular meetings with clients to help assess job performance, address concerns, and provide constructive feedback. If necessary, job coaches can create and implement performance improvement plans, setting clear and achievable goals.

Skill Development

To ensure job success, job coaches can provide hands-on training to develop both job-specific and some basic, but essential soft skills, such as:

- Communication
- Teamwork
- Problem-solving
- Time management
- Performance monitoring and feedback

Employer Collaboration

In cases job coaches have partnerships with employers for work experience or supported employment services, educating employers about the needs of their employees fosters a more inclusive workplace. Job coaches should facilitate open communication between employers and clients to ensure understanding and cooperation.

Accessibility and Accommodations

For clients with disabilities, job coaches collaborate with employers to arrange reasonable accommodations. They also introduce assistive technologies and provide training to enhance job performance.

Problem-Solving and Conflict Resolution

In cases of workplace conflicts, job coaches who facilitate job placement services, can act as mediators, facilitating communication and resolution strategies. They help clients manage challenges and stress, ensuring they handle workplace issues proactively.

Building Independence

As clients gain confidence in their roles, job coaches gradually reduce direct support, empowering individuals to advocate for themselves and seek resources independently.

LONG-TERM CAREER SUCCESS

Achieving long-term career success requires continuous development, strategic planning, and resilience. Here are key strategies to support clients in building sustainable careers.

Goal Setting and Career Planning

Work with clients to identify their long-term career aspirations and set both short-term and long-term goals. Help clients map out a clear career pathway, outlining steps and milestones needed to achieve their objectives.

Skill Development

Encourage lifelong learning through courses, certifications, and training programs. Regularly assess skills gaps and provide resources or opportunities for professional growth.

Networking and Support Systems

Building a strong professional network is key to long-term success. Help clients establish peer support systems within the workplace and connect them with external resources and support groups for ongoing personal and professional development. Help clients connect with mentors who can provide guidance and career development insights.

Personal Branding

Some careers can benefit from developing a strong personal brand that highlights their strengths, values, and professional identity. Help clients create and maintain a professional online presence, including LinkedIn profiles and personal websites.

Career Resilience and Adaptability

Teach clients how to develop resilience to navigate setbacks and career challenges. Encourage flexibility and adaptability to keep up with changes in industry trends and the job market.

Effective Job Search Strategies

Continue to provide training on job search techniques, including resume writing, interview skills, and leveraging job search platforms. Teach clients how to access the hidden job market through networking and proactive outreach.

Work-Life Balance and Well-Being

Emphasize the importance of work-life balance and guide clients in managing stress effectively. Encourage self-care practices to maintain both professional performance and personal well-being.

Performance and Feedback

Coach clients on how to seek and utilize employer feedback constructively for career growth. Encourage regular self-assessment to reflect on achievements and areas for improvement.

Leadership and Management Development

Provide leadership development opportunities through workshops, seminars, and hands-on experiences. Offer training in management skills for clients aspiring to transition into supervisory or managerial roles.

Career Transitions

Support clients in navigating career transitions, whether shifting industries, changing roles, or starting a business. Help clients identify and leverage transferable skills applicable to new roles or industries.

Market Awareness and Industry Trends

Keep clients informed about industry trends, emerging technologies, and job market changes. Educate them on economic factors that may impact career opportunities and strategies to stay competitive.

Feedback and Accountability

Lastly, schedule regular check-ins to review progress, set new goals, and adjust career strategies as needed. Act as an accountability partner, ensuring clients stay on track with their career plans and professional development.

COMMON EMPLOYER EXPECTATIONS

Ensure that your client understands basic employer expectations. Expectations vary, but most workplaces require employees to demonstrate professionalism, respect, and accountability. Workplace etiquette refers to a set of behaviors that foster a positive, productive, and respectful work environment.

Punctuality

- Arrive on time for work, meetings, and appointments.
- Being punctual demonstrates reliability and respect for others' time.

Professional Appearance

- Dress appropriately according to the company's dress code.
- Maintain good personal hygiene to present a professional image.

Respectful Communication

- Speak and write clearly, courteously, and professionally.
- Listen actively, avoid interrupting, and be mindful of tone and body language.

Email and Phone Etiquette

- Respond to emails and phone calls promptly and professionally.
- Use proper email formatting and keep phone conversations brief and relevant.

Confidentiality

- Respect the privacy and confidentiality of company information and conversations.
- Avoid sharing sensitive information with unauthorized individuals.

Workspace Maintenance

- Keep your work area clean and organized.
- Respect shared spaces and equipment by maintaining cleanliness and order.

Collaboration and Teamwork

- Work cooperatively with colleagues, offering help and support when needed.
- Respect different opinions and work styles to promote a harmonious workplace.

Positive Attitude

- Maintain professionalism and composure, even in challenging situations.
- Approach problems with a solution-oriented mindset.

Feedback and Recognition

- Give and receive constructive feedback graciously.
- Acknowledge and appreciate the contributions of colleagues.

Professionalism in Meetings

- Prepare in advance, participate actively, and follow the agenda.
- Stay focused and avoid distractions, such as checking your phone.

Adherence to Policies

- Follow company policies and procedures, including those related to safety, conduct, and use of company resources.

Respecting Boundaries

- Maintain professional and personal boundaries in the workplace.
- Avoid overly personal conversations or behaviors that may make others uncomfortable.

WORKPLACE CONFLICT

Workplace conflicts and challenges are an inevitable part of professional life. At some point, everyone encounters difficulties at work. These challenges can often be effectively resolved through communication, empathy, and problem-solving skills, fostering a more harmonious and productive work environment. Your client may be an employee or a supervisor, and the advice or resources you provide will depend on their specific situation.

Here are some effective strategies for managing workplace conflict.

Open Communication

When resolving a conflict, ensure all parties feel heard by actively listening to their concerns without interruption. This fosters understanding of the root cause. All individuals should express their viewpoints clearly and respectfully, focusing on facts and feelings rather than placing blame.

Empathy and Understanding

Acknowledge the perspectives and emotions of others involved in the conflict. Demonstrating empathy can help defuse tension and promote cooperation. Validate others' emotions by recognizing their feelings without necessarily agreeing with their viewpoint.

Identify the Root Cause

Look beyond the immediate issue to uncover underlying causes such as miscommunication, differing values, or resource limitations. Use open-ended questions to gather information and gain deeper insight into the situation.

Collaborative Problem-Solving

Encourage all parties to contribute ideas and brainstorm potential solutions together. Evaluate the pros and cons of each solution and strive for a compromise that addresses key concerns.

Establish Common Goals

Identify shared objectives that all parties can support, shifting the focus from individual grievances to collective benefits. Emphasize teamwork and how resolving conflicts can lead to better outcomes for the organization.

Set Clear Boundaries and Expectations

Define acceptable workplace behavior to help prevent future conflicts. Establish ground rules for discussions to ensure a respectful and productive environment.

Seek Mediation

For particularly complex or intense conflicts, involve a neutral third-party mediator to facilitate resolution. If internal mediation is unsuccessful, external professional mediators can provide structured support.

Follow-Up and Monitor

After resolving the conflict, schedule follow-up meetings to assess progress and address any emerging issues. Monitor workplace relationships to identify and mitigate potential recurring conflicts early.

Develop Conflict Resolution Skills

Engage in conflict resolution and communication training to build the skills needed for constructive dispute management. Use role-playing exercises to practice handling conflicts, increasing confidence and competence.

Promote a Positive Work Environment

Foster an inclusive workplace culture where diversity is valued, and employees feel respected and supported. Encourage collaboration and team-building activities to strengthen relationships and minimize conflicts.

Document and Reflect

Maintain records of conflicts and resolutions to identify patterns and areas for improvement. Reflect on the conflict resolution process to recognize what worked well and what can be enhanced in future situations.

RESOURCES FOR JOB COACHES

- US Equal Employment Opportunity Commission
  https://www.eeoc.gov/

13

Career Planning

- Job Coach vs Career Counselor
- The 4 Steps of Career Planning
- Resources for Job Coaches

JOB COACH VS CAREER COUNSELOR

Job coaches and career counselors both offer guidance and support to individuals seeking employment or career advancement, but their focus, approach, and scope of services differ. Job coaches primarily assist with practical job search skills to help individuals secure immediate employment, while career counselors take a holistic approach, emphasizing career exploration, planning, and long-term professional development.

Job Coach

A job coach works directly with individuals to help them secure and sustain employment.

They focus on the practical aspects of job searching and employment, including resume writing, interview preparation, job search strategies, and on-the-job training.

They often assist individuals facing specific employment challenges, such as those with disabilities, justice-involved individuals, or career changers.

They provide hands-on support, job placement assistance, and ongoing guidance to help individuals succeed in their chosen jobs or careers.

Career Counselor

A career counselor takes a comprehensive approach to career development, helping individuals explore and manage their careers over the long term.

They assess clients' interests, skills, values, and goals to support informed career decisions and strategic career planning.

Career counselors provide guidance on various career-related topics, including career exploration, educational pathways, skill development, job search strategies, and career advancement.

They work in diverse settings such as schools, colleges, universities, career centers, and private practices, serving clients of all ages and backgrounds.

Utilizing assessments, counseling techniques, and career development theories, career counselors help individuals clarify their career goals and navigate transitions throughout their professional journeys.

A *Career* can be defined as *"more than just a job, a chosen profession or occupation in which you work in and develop over an extended period, with the intention of progressing, growing, achieving success and expertise in that field."*

A career could involve:

- Long Term Commitment
- Professional Growth
- Goals and Aspirations
- Continued Learning
- Specialization
- Job Stability
- Income & Financial Stability
- Networking
- Job Satisfaction
- Contribution to Society
- Passion and Sense of Purpose

THE 4 STEPS OF CAREER PLANNING

Step 1 Self-Reflection

Self-Reflection is the process of introspectively examining and evaluating one's thoughts, feelings, behaviors, and experiences. In career planning, self-reflection helps individuals make more informed personal and professional decisions.

When self-reflecting, we can ask ourselves questions like:

- *What kind of tasks do I enjoy doing?*
- *What tasks do I prefer not to do?*
- *What work environments do I prefer to work in?*
- *What am I good at?*
- *What skills do I have?*
- *What types of jobs or careers do I want to explore?*

After self-reflecting it's recommended to take two different career aptitude or personality tests, as discussed in Chapter 2.

Step 2 Choose a Career(s) to Explore

Career Exploration helps individuals identify fields that align with their interests, strengths, and skills, leading to greater job satisfaction and performance. In this step, the individual should gather detailed information about the specific career they are considering.

...Before deciding on a career, it is key to learn about the educational and training requirements for the job. Requirements may include degrees, certificates, licenses, apprenticeships, work experience, passing of exams, digital badges, etc.

1. Conduct Online Research

www.Onetonline.org A reliable website can provide valuable insights into job duties, work environments, requirements, wages, job vacancies, training programs, and industry associations related to specific careers. State labor departments or workforce agencies typically maintain labor market information websites, offering data on labor market trends, demand for specific roles, salary expectations, and future job prospects.

Labor Market Information is discussed in Chapter 14.

2. Conduct Informational Interviews

Engage with professionals in the industry, company, or profession of interest through informational interviews. Speaking with experienced individuals provides first-hand knowledge, career insights, and a deeper understanding of job expectations and industry trends.

3. Review Job Postings

Examine real job listings to identify common employer requirements, qualifications, and skills needed for various roles. This helps job seekers align their experience and training with industry expectations.

*Complete a Career Exploration Worksheet.

Step 3 Explore Training Programs

All careers require some form of training, whether through formal education or on-the-job experience. If a job requires a degree or certification, it's important to explore various schools and programs. Before deciding, students should research and compare different colleges, universities, or training programs to ensure they make an informed choice.

Important things to consider

- Duration of the program
- Credentials offered
- Start dates/schedules

- Cost of tuition/fees
- Job placement
- School programs, clubs and campus activities
- Housing options

*Complete a Training Exploration Worksheet

Step 4 Set Goals and Make a Game Plan

Understanding the specific requirements for the desired job or career will help determine the goals that need to be set.

Career Exploration Worksheet

Career: ____

Description of occupation: ____

____

____

____

____

Tasks performed: ____

____

____

____

____

Educational/Skills Requirements: ____

____

____

____

Wages information: ____

____

____

____

Labor market trends & outlooks: ____

____

____

Type of work (full-time, part-time, seasonal, contract, etc.)

Other things you learned about this career:

Professional organizations associated with this industry:

Training Exploration Worksheet

School

Location / Contact Info

Programs, Degrees, Certifications

Requirements

Duration of the Program

Important Dates

____
____
____
Cost of Tuition ____
____
____
____

Other Information: (accreditation, graduation rate, job placement assistance, student groups, reviews, housing options) ______________________________
____
____
____

Career Game Plan Worksheet

Client Information

Name:

Date:

Job Coach:

Career Objective: *(Example: "To secure a full-time administrative assistant position within the healthcare industry.")*

---

1. Skills & Strengths

- **Current Skills:** *(Relevant to the career objective.)*
- **Personal Strengths: Areas for Improvement:** *(Identify any skills or qualifications that need improvement or development)*

2. Career Goals

Short-Term Goals (1-6 Months)

- Goal 1:
- Goal 2:
- Goal 3:

Mid-Term Goals (6-12 Months)

- Goal 1:
- Goal 2:

Long-Term Goals (1-3 Years)

- Goal 1:
- Goal 2:

---

3. Action Steps

For each goal, list specific, achievable action steps that the client can take. Include a timeline and any resources needed.

Goal	Action Step	Timeline	Resources Needed

---

4. Networking & Support

- **Networking Contacts:** *(List people, organizations that could provide guidance, mentoring, or job leads, such as career fairs, LinkedIn groups, or networking events.)*

- **Support System:** *(Identify friends, family, or mentors who can provide support throughout the job search process.)*

---

5. Training & Education

- **Required Training:** *(Any specific certifications, courses, or training needed for the career goal)*
- **Resources:** *(Institutions, online courses, or programs that offer the necessary training)*
- **Timeline:** *(Target dates for completing training or educational steps)*

---

6. Job Search Plan

Job Search Strategies:

- **Preferred Industries:** *(List industries that align with career goals)*
- **Target Employers:** *(List potential companies or employers)*
- **Job Search Tools:** *(Websites, job boards, social media, or networking platforms)*

Application Goals: *(Example: Apply to 3-5 jobs per week)*

7. Mock Interview Preparation

- **Interview Practice Sessions:** *(Dates for scheduled mock interviews)*
- **Common Interview Questions:** *(List questions that may come up specific to their field)*
- **Personalized Answers & STAR Stories:** *(Create STAR responses for common interview questions)*

8. Tracking Progress & Reflection

Weekly/Monthly Check-Ins:

- **Date:**
- **Progress on Goals:** *(Discuss achievements, areas of improvement, or adjustments needed)*
- **New Challenges or Insights:** *(Reflect on any obstacles faced or lessons learned)*

---

9. Success Markers

Define success indicators that show when each goal or milestone is achieved. This can help the client recognize and celebrate progress.

- **Examples of Success Markers:** "Completed certification," "Scheduled three informational interviews," and "Secured a first-round interview."

10. Final Reflection & Adjustment

Review & Adjustments: *(Date)*

- **What's Working Well:**
- **Adjustments Needed:**

Final Thoughts: *(Client's reflections on their journey and insights gained)*

RESOURCES FOR JOB COACHES

Occupational Information and Data

- Bureau of Labor Statistics www.bls.gov
- ONET Online www.onetonline.org

Media/TV

- Dirty Jobs https://discovery.com/shows/dirty-jobs
- The College Tour www.thecollegetour.com

14

The Labor Market

- The Labor Market
- Best Practices
- High Demand Industries
- Resources for Job Coaches

THE LABOR MARKET

The *Labor Market* refers to the availability of employment and labor, based on supply and demand—workers provide labor, while employers offer jobs. A "local" labor market may refer to the workforce conditions within a specific county or region. The labor market is a key economic factor, influencing employment levels, working hours, and wages.

Importance of Labor Market Information (LMI)

Labor Market Information (LMI) is essential for job seekers, employers, policymakers, and educators.

For job seekers, LMI helps individuals make informed career and educational decisions by aligning their skills with current and future market demands.

For employers, it supports strategic workforce planning, allowing businesses to anticipate talent gaps and remain competitive.

For policymakers and educators, LMI guides the development of workforce training programs and curricula to meet evolving economic needs.

Government agencies, such as the U.S. Bureau of Labor Statistics (BLS) and state labor departments, offer detailed reports on national and regional labor markets. Additionally, online job boards (e.g., LinkedIn, Indeed, Glassdoor) provide real-time data on job postings and employer requirements. Industry associations, professional organizations, economic research firms, and consulting companies also publish labor market analyses and forecasts.

Labor markets vary by state and county, making it important for job seekers to understand LMI specific to their region. Generally, there will be local training programs available for the high-demand occupations in the region to help individuals develop the necessary skills for these roles.

Factors that Affect the Employment Landscape

The employment landscape evolves over time due to factors such as technological advancements, economic shifts, and societal changes. By staying informed about these trends and the top industries in demand, job coaches can provide accurate, timely, and strategic guidance, increasing their clients' chances of securing employment.

Geographic location and climate significantly influence a state's labor market by shaping key industries and job opportunities. States with favorable climates and diverse landscapes, such as California and Florida, often have thriving tourism, agriculture, and outdoor recreation sectors, creating employment in hospitality, farming, and entertainment. In contrast, regions with harsher climates may focus on industries like energy production—such as oil, gas, and renewable energy—leveraging natural resources while addressing environmental challenges. Additionally, geographic factors impact the presence of major transportation hubs, tech corridors, and manufacturing centers, influencing industry growth and the demand for specific skill sets.

BEST PRACTICES

By staying informed about industry trends, required qualifications, and specific job roles, job coaches can identify suitable opportunities and prepare clients for the demands of their chosen fields. Familiarity with labor market data—such as unemployment rates, job vacancy trends, and wage statistics—helps coaches set realistic expectations and develop effective job search strategies. Additionally, in-depth industry knowledge enhances a coach's credibility, fostering trust and improving client outcomes.

Current Job Market Trends

Understanding which industries are expanding and which are declining allows job coaches to guide clients toward stable and promising career paths.

In-Demand Skills and Qualifications

Identifying high-demand skills and qualifications across industries helps coaches recommend relevant training and certification programs.

Geographic Employment Patterns

Being aware of regional job opportunities and industry hubs enables coaches to advise clients on the best locations for job searches or potential relocation.

Remote Work Trends

Understanding the growing prevalence of remote work and its impact on different industries helps coaches prepare clients for virtual job markets and remote employment opportunities.

Emerging Industries

Monitoring the rise of sectors such as renewable energy, biotechnology, and artificial intelligence provides clients with insights into future job opportunities and necessary skill sets.

Industry-Specific Challenges and Opportunities

Recognizing the unique challenges and growth potential in various industries allows coaches to offer targeted advice and tailored solutions to clients.

Networking and Professional Associations

Awareness of key professional associations, industry events, and networking opportunities helps coaches connect clients with valuable resources and contacts.

HIGH DEMAND INDUSTRIES

With the rapid evolution of technology, several industries in the United States consistently experience strong demand for skilled professionals. While trends may shift due to technological advancements, economic changes, and societal factors, the following sectors have demonstrated resilience and sustained growth.

Many of these industries that have been historically in high demand:

- Technology
- Healthcare
- Finance and Accounting
- Education
- Skilled Trades
- Green Energy
- Digital Marketing and Media
- Logistics and Supply Chain Management
- Biotechnology and Pharmaceutical
- Engineering

Technology

The demand for professionals in software engineering, data science, cybersecurity, artificial intelligence, and cloud computing remains strong as businesses continue to embrace digital transformation.

Healthcare

An aging population and advancements in medical treatments drive the continuous need for healthcare professionals, including physicians, nurses, allied health specialists, medical technologists, and healthcare administrators.

Finance and Accounting

Financial institutions, corporations, and accounting firms seek experts in finance, accounting, auditing, and financial analysis to manage investments, regulatory compliance, and financial planning.

Engineering

Engineers play vital roles across industries such as aerospace, civil, mechanical, electrical, and computer engineering. Skilled engineers are in high demand to design, innovate, and maintain infrastructure and technology.

Education

The need for skilled educators, administrators, and specialists remains strong in both K-12 and higher education to support growing student populations and evolving educational initiatives.

Skilled Trades

Electricians, plumbers, HVAC technicians, and construction workers are essential to infrastructure development, maintenance, and renovations, ensuring continued demand for skilled tradespeople.

Green Energy

Growing concerns about climate change have fueled demand for professionals in renewable energy sectors such as solar, wind, and hydroelectric power, along with energy efficiency and sustainability roles.

Digital Marketing and Media

As businesses expand their digital presence, professionals skilled in digital marketing, social media management, content creation, and analytics are increasingly sought after.

Biotechnology and Pharmaceuticals

Advancements in medical research and drug development have heightened the demand for professionals in biotechnology, pharmaceuticals, and life sciences, including researchers, lab technicians, and regulatory affairs specialists.

Logistics and Supply Chain Management

With the rise of e-commerce and global trade, experts in logistics, supply chain management, and distribution are essential to ensuring efficient operations and delivery networks.

High Demand Occupations

Across all 50 states, the healthcare and technology sectors continue to experience high demand. Each state faces a critical need for workers in at least three of the following ten in-demand occupations:

- Data Scientist
- Software Developer
- Registered Nurse
- Truck Driver
- Manufacturing Worker
- Construction Laborer
- Medical Assistant
- Personal Care Aide/Home Health Aide
- Retail Salesperson
- Food Service Worker

20 Computer Science Jobs

These roles cover a wide range of specializations within the field of Computer Science, offering various opportunities based on interests and skills.

- Software Developer/Engineer
- Data Scientist
- Web Developer
- Database Administrator
- Systems Analyst
- Network Engineer
- Cybersecurity Analyst
- Machine Learning Engineer
- Artificial Intelligence (AI) Engineer
- Cloud Architect
- Mobile App Developer
- DevOps Engineer
- IT Project Manager
- Software Quality Assurance (QA) Engineer
- Computer Systems Engineer
- Game Developer
- IT Support Specialist
- Blockchain Developer
- Embedded Systems Engineer
- Computer Science Researcher

RESOURCES FOR JOB SEEKERS

Occupational Information and Data

- Bureau of Labor Statistics www.bls.gov
- ONET Online www.onetonline.org

15

Professional Development

- Professional Development
- Personal Development
- Human Capital
- Social Capital
- Dimensions of Wellness
- An Industry Expert
- Resources for Job Coaches

Both professional and personal development play essential roles in an individual's growth. While they focus on different areas, they often overlap, as skills and qualities gained in one area can benefit the other. A balanced approach contributes to holistic growth and a more fulfilling life.

For example, personal development enhances emotional intelligence, improving professional relationships and performance. Likewise, professional skills such as time management can lead to greater efficiency and reduced stress in an individual's personal life.

PROFESSIONAL DEVELOPMENT

Professional Development is the ongoing process of acquiring new skills, knowledge, and experiences directly related to one's career. It aims to improve job performance, advance career opportunities, and keep individuals up to date with industry trends.

Here are some ways to foster professional development.

Career Planning

Set clear goals and develop a plan to achieve them.

Career Planning is discussed in Chapter 13.

Performance Improvement

Seek regular feedback and evaluations to identify areas for growth and track progress. Engaging in professional mentorship can provide valuable guidance and support.

Research and Innovation

Contribute to your field by conducting research and developing new methods, products, or solutions that address industry challenges.

Staying Passionate

Work on projects that align with your interests to maintain motivation, enthusiasm, and long-term career satisfaction.

Maintaining Work-Life Balance

Prioritize a healthy balance between work and personal life to sustain productivity and prevent burnout.

PERSONAL DEVELOPMENT

Personal Development focuses on self-improvement across various aspects of life, including emotional, intellectual, physical, and social well-being. It aims to enhance self-awareness, personal fulfillment, and overall quality of life.

Here are some aspects of personal development.

Emotional Intelligence

Develop a deeper understanding of emotions and improve emotional management.

Self-Awareness

Gain insights into personal values, beliefs, and behaviors to foster growth.

Health and Wellness

Prioritize physical health and overall well-being through self-care practices, such as reading self-help books, practicing mindfulness or meditation, and engaging in regular exercise.

Lifelong Learning

Pursue new knowledge and interests beyond professional development, such as learning a new language, exploring hobbies, or participating in personal counseling or coaching.

Relationship Building

Strengthen personal relationships and social skills to enhance meaningful connections.

HUMAN CAPITAL

Human Capital encompasses the skills, knowledge, education, and experience individuals acquire, enhancing their ability to work efficiently, boost productivity, and drive economic growth. It develops through investments in education, training, and health, serving as a crucial determinant of employability, earning potential, and career progression.

Here are some things that can contribute to human capital.

Continuous Learning and Skill Enhancement

Stay ahead in your field by mastering new tools, techniques, and methodologies. Enroll in courses and webinars relevant to your profession and pursue advanced degrees or certifications that align with your industry. Regularly read industry journals, blogs, books, and research publications to stay informed about the latest trends and developments.

Certifications and Training

Enhance your credentials by obtaining industry-recognized certifications and attending workshops or seminars. Participate in job-specific training programs to deepen your expertise and remain competitive in your field.

Practical Experience

Build extensive hands-on experience by taking on diverse roles within your industry. Tackle challenging projects that push your boundaries and expand your skill set. Engage in internships or volunteer work to gain practical exposure and a broader perspective.

Skill Development

Master industry-standard tools, technologies, and methodologies. Strengthen essential soft skills such as communication, leadership, problem-solving, and critical thinking. If applicable, learn new languages to enhance your ability to engage with a global audience.

Mentorship and Teaching

Give back to your industry by mentoring junior professionals and students. Share your expertise by teaching courses or leading workshops relevant to your field.

Building a Personal Brand

Establish a strong professional presence through social media, a personal website, or a blog. Actively network with peers, thought leaders, and potential collaborators both online and in person. Leverage media opportunities to position yourself as a respected expert in your industry.

Thought Leadership

Contribute valuable insights by writing articles, research papers, or books on topics related to your field. Launch a blog to share your experiences and knowledge with a broader audience, establishing yourself as a thought leader.

SOCIAL CAPITAL

Social Capital encompasses the networks, relationships, and connections individuals cultivate within their community, workplace, and society. These relationships provide access to resources, information, support, and opportunities that contribute to personal and professional growth. Built on trust, cooperation, and mutual exchange, social capital plays a vital role in achieving success.

Here are some things that can contribute to social capital.

Networking

Building professional relationships expand your network by connecting with professionals in your field to exchange knowledge and opportunities. Attend industry conferences, seminars, and networking events to stay informed and engaged. Join professional organizations and actively participate in their activities. Speak at conferences, workshops, and panels to share insights and establish credibility. Seek guidance from experienced mentors and industry experts to accelerate your growth.

Feedback and Continuous Improvement

Regularly seek constructive feedback from peers, mentors, and industry leaders. Continuously assess your skills and knowledge to identify areas for improvement and professional development.

Collaboration

Work with professionals from related fields to gain fresh perspectives and insights. Engage in collaborative projects that require diverse skill sets and expertise. Participate in public speaking opportunities, such as webinars, podcasts, and industry events, to share your expertise and expand your influence.

The Interconnection of Social and Human Capital

Both social and human capital are essential for individual and societal growth. Social capital facilitates access to opportunities, while human capital empowers individuals to maximize those opportunities, driving personal *and* professional success.

THE DIMENSIONS OF WELLNESS

The Dimensions of Wellness concept has evolved over time, gaining recognition through the contributions of various individuals and organizations. Dr. Bill Hettler and the National Wellness Institute (NWI) are often credited with developing and popularizing the 6- and 8-dimension wellness models.

The *8 Dimensions of Wellness* provide a holistic approach to health, acknowledging that well-being extends beyond just physical health.

These dimensions include Physical, Emotional, Social, Intellectual, Occupational, Environmental. Financial, and Spiritual Wellness.

Addressing each dimension fosters a well-rounded approach to personal growth and well-being. Prioritizing these areas helps individuals achieve overall life satisfaction, build resilience against challenges, unlock their full potential, and maintain a healthy, fulfilling, and productive life.

Physical Wellness

Maintaining physical health through regular exercise, proper nutrition, adequate sleep, and routine medical check-ups is essential for overall well-being.

- Boosts energy levels and enhances overall vitality.
- Reduces the risk of chronic diseases and promotes longevity.
- Supports mental health by alleviating stress and anxiety.

Emotional Wellness

Developing the ability to understand and manage emotions effectively, cope with stress, and build resilience is essential for overall well-being.

- Enhances self-awareness and strengthens emotional intelligence.
- Improves relationships by fostering better communication and connection.
- Promotes mental stability and reduces the risk of mental health challenges.

Intellectual Wellness

Engaging in lifelong learning, critical thinking, and creative pursuits:

- Encourages curiosity and open-mindedness.
- Enhances problem-solving skills and fosters innovation.
- Sharpens the mind and helps prevent cognitive decline.

Social Wellness

Building healthy, supportive relationships and a strong social network:

- Provides emotional support and fosters a sense of belonging.
- Enhances communication and interpersonal skills.
- Reduces feelings of loneliness and isolation.

Spiritual Wellness

Finding purpose, meaning, and connection to something greater than oneself:

- Fosters inner peace and contentment.
- Provides a sense of purpose and direction in life.
- Encourages values and ethics that guide behavior and decision-making.

Environmental Wellness

Living in harmony with the environment and promoting sustainability:

- Supports a healthy and safe living environment.
- Encourages sustainable practices and respect for nature.
- Enhances overall well-being by reducing environmental stressors.

Financial Wellness

Managing finances effectively, planning for future security, and living within one's means:

- Reduces financial stress and anxiety.
- Strengthens the ability to make informed financial decisions.
- Provides security and freedom to pursue personal and professional goals.

Occupational Wellness

Finding fulfillment in work and maintaining a healthy work-life balance:

- Increases job satisfaction and career growth.
- Reduces work-related stress and burnout.
- Enhances overall life satisfaction and productivity.

Occupational wellness plays a crucial role in overall well-being and quality of life. A fulfilling and balanced work life contributes to emotional wellness by reducing stress and enhancing job satisfaction, while also supporting financial wellness through stable income and financial security. The intellectual challenges and opportunities for growth at work promote intellectual wellness, and positive workplace relationships strengthen social wellness. Additionally, a healthy work-life balance allows individuals to engage in physical wellness activities, such as exercise and rest, while also fostering spiritual and environmental wellness by aligning work with personal values and sustainable practices.

By achieving occupational wellness, individuals create a strong foundation that integrates and enhances all other dimensions of wellness.

As job coaches, our primary role is to help clients gain employment—we are not health or life coaches. However, it's important to recognize that these dimensions of wellness are interconnected and collectively contribute to a balanced and fulfilling life. For example, when an individual's mental, physical, and financial health are in good standing, they are better equipped to work and successfully achieve their occupational and life goals.

AN INDUSTRY EXPERT

Becoming a recognized expert in your industry requires a combination of continuous learning, hands-on experience, networking, and knowledge-sharing.

Start by building a strong educational foundation, whether through a relevant degree, certification, or specialized training. Develop practical skills by gaining experience through internships, entry-level roles, or freelance work. Networking is essential—attend industry conferences, join professional associations, and connect with mentors and peers to stay updated on trends and innovations.

Commit to lifelong learning by reading industry publications, enrolling in advanced courses, and participating in workshops and webinars. Finally, establish yourself as a thought leader by sharing your expertise—write articles, speak at events, and contribute to online forums. By consistently refining your knowledge and engaging with your industry, you can position yourself as a trusted authority in your field.

The Importance

Becoming an industry expert offers numerous advantages that can elevate both career success and personal growth. Experts are highly sought after for their deep knowledge and specialized skills, leading to increased job opportunities, higher salaries, and greater job security. They are often invited to speak at conferences, contribute to industry publications, and consult on high-profile projects, further enhancing their professional reputation and visibility.

Beyond career benefits, industry experts have the opportunity to shape standards and practices, driving innovation and meaningful change. Mastering a field also brings a sense of fulfillment and confidence, allowing experts to make valuable contributions that advance their industry and inspire others.

RESOURCES FOR JOB COACHES

- Center on Integrated Health Care & Self-Directed Recovery

  https://www.center4healthandsdc.org/wellness-in-8d.html
- National Wellness Institute https://nationalwellness.org/

16

A Catalyst for Change

- Developing Partnerships and Collaborations
- Closing Message

Chapter 2 explored assessments and goal setting, Chapters 7 through 11 focused on working with special populations, and Chapter 15 covered personal and professional development.

At its core, it's all about growth, improvement, and change.

Ultimately, it's about helping people.

DEVELOPING PARTNERSHIPS AND COLLABORATIONS

One of the most valuable skills for a Job Coach is the ability to share resources with clients and refer them to professionals who can assist with other areas of life. Developing strong community partnerships is essential for providing comprehensive support and access to vital resources.

The availability of services varies by region—major cities often offer more programs but also have a higher demand for human services. By actively connecting with local organizations and professionals, job coaches can better support their clients while also enhancing their own professional development.

...Signing up for newsletters is a great way to keep informed about upcoming events, resources, etc. For example, newsletters from state and county workforce development boards.

Identify Potential Partners

Local Businesses: Establish partnerships with businesses that offer employment opportunities, internships, and job shadowing experiences for clients.

Educational Institutions: Collaborate with schools, colleges, and vocational training centers to connect clients with training programs and educational resources.

Nonprofit Organizations: Collaborate with local nonprofits that provide employment-related. Partner with organizations that address additional client needs to offer more comprehensive support.

Networking

Attend Community Events: Participate in job fairs, business expos, networking meetings, and local events to connect with potential partners and raise awareness about your services.

Join Professional Associations: Become a member of local and regional professional associations focused on career development and workforce training to expand your network and stay informed on industry trends.

Leverage Social Media and Online Platforms

LinkedIn: Connect with local businesses, community leaders, and organizations. Share updates and success stories to showcase your work and attract potential partners.

Community Forums: Engage in online forums and groups where potential partners are active to build relationships and expand your network.

Offer Mutual Benefits

Highlight Mutual Goals: Emphasize the shared benefits of collaboration, such as helping businesses find qualified employees or providing students with hands-on job experience.

Share Resources: Offer workshops, training sessions, or other valuable resources to support partner organizations and strengthen the relationship.

Create Collaborative Programs

Joint Workshops and Training: Partner with organizations to develop and offer workshops or training programs that provide clients with enhanced learning opportunities.

Internship and Apprenticeship Programs: Collaborate with local businesses to create internship and apprenticeship opportunities, giving clients valuable hands-on experience.

Engage in Community Service

Volunteer Work: Engage in community service projects and encourage clients to participate. Volunteering fosters goodwill, strengthens community ties, and creates valuable networking opportunities.

Local Boards and Committees: Serve on workforce development and community improvement boards or committees to expand your influence and contribute to meaningful change.

Organize Community Events

Job Fairs: Collaborate with local businesses and organizations to host job fairs, providing clients with direct access to potential employers.

Career Days: Organize career days at schools and community centers to offer career guidance and showcase diverse professional opportunities.

Communication and Outreach

Regular Updates: Keep partners engaged by sharing newsletters, emails, and meetings that highlight successes, upcoming events, and collaboration opportunities.

Personalized Outreach: Customize your communication to align with each partner's interests and needs, demonstrating the mutual benefits of collaboration.

Establish Formal Agreements

Memoranda of Understanding (MOUs): Establish MOUs to formalize partnerships, clearly defining the roles and responsibilities of each party.

Partnership Agreements: Develop detailed agreements for structured collaborations, outlining goals, activities, and evaluation methods.

Measuring and Showcasing Success

Track Outcomes: Assess the impact of partnerships on client success, including employment rates, skill development, and job retention.

Share Success Stories: Highlight successful collaborations and client achievements through reports, newsletters, and social media to showcase the value of partnerships.

Continuous Improvement

Feedback Loops: Implement regular feedback mechanisms with partners to enhance collaboration and address concerns proactively.

Adapt and Evolve: Continuously refine partnership strategies based on feedback and evolving community needs.

CLOSING MESSAGE

As you embark on your journey as a professional job coach, remember that your role extends beyond guiding clients toward employment—it is about empowering them to envision and achieve their fullest potential. You will work with individuals from diverse backgrounds, each with unique stories, challenges, and aspirations. Your empathy, resilience, and unwavering commitment to their success will serve as the foundation for their growth and transformation.

Never underestimate the impact of your encouragement, the value of your insights, and the strength of your advocacy. Every resume you help refine, every interview you help prepare for, and every barrier you help clients overcome contributes to a larger narrative of hope and opportunity. Your dedication does more than build careers—it helps shape lives filled with purpose and direction.

The economic significance of employment cannot be overstated. When individuals work and thrive, the benefits extend far beyond personal success. A high employment rate strengthens communities and nations by increasing productivity, boosting tax revenues, and reducing reliance on social welfare programs. This economic vitality supports public services, infrastructure investments, and an overall higher quality of life. When individuals achieve financial stability, they create a cycle of growth and prosperity that benefits society as a whole.

In closing, embrace the continuous learning and growth this profession demands. Stay curious, remain compassionate, and strive to understand the evolving job market and the needs of those you serve. Your work as a job coach holds the power to change lives—one meaningful career at a time. Carry this responsibility with pride and passion, knowing that you are a catalyst for positive change in the world of work. ~Thank you for choosing this path and for making a difference in the lives of so many.